The Little Network Book

Lon Poole and John Rizzo

Illustrations by John Grimes

Peachpit Press
Berkeley ▼ California

Peachpit Press
1249 Eighth Street
Berkeley, CA 94710
510 524 2178
fax 510 524 2221
Find us on the Web at http://www.peachpit.com

The Little Network Book

Peachpit Press is a division of Addison Wesley Longman

Editors: Lisa Theobald, Judy Ziajka
Production Coordinator: Amy Changar
Compositor: Owen Wolfson
Interior Design: Robin Williams
Cover Design: **TMA** Ted Mader Associates
Cartoon Illustrations: John Grimes
Indexer: Karin Arrigoni

ISBN 0-201-35378-4

0 9 8 7 6 5 4 3 2 1
Printed and bound in the United States of America

Acknowledgments

We'd like to thank our editor, Lisa Theobald, for helping us develop this book while patiently and persistently pushing it to completion. We never would have finished without you. Thanks to Carol Henry, copy editor, for making our writing so much easier to read. Thanks to Amy Changar for quickly and efficiently coordinating the production process. Thanks also to Owen Wolfson for an ingenious job of page layout. And thank you, John Grimes, for your inspired illustrations.

Lon would like to thank his family for their loving support during the writing of this book. Thanks, Ethan and Adam, for letting me use "the Windows" so much. Thank you so much, Karin, for giving me the time to do this, and for listening.

John would like to thank Christine and Adriana for their patience.

Contents

Work and Play   87

Read Me First

Imagine your reaction a few of years ago if someone had told you that you would have more than one computer in your home or small office and that you would connect them in a network. Back then, you probably thought of a network as a huge, complicated system that required lots of work and administration to use. Today, however, the idea of a small network with two or three computers isn't so outlandish. You probably know that there are benefits to using a network, but you're not exactly sure just what those benefits are and you don't know what kind of effort and expense is involved in setting up and using a network.

We're here to tell you that you don't need a degree in computer science or a corporate bankroll to put together your own small network. If you can follow directions and have $50 to $100 to spend on cables and such, you can easily connect a few computers in a network and do something useful and fun with it. This book tells you how.

In describing how to set up and operate a small network, we assume you know nothing or very little about networks. We tell you exactly what you need to know and what you need to do, and we leave out all the confusing technical details that you don't have to know to get your network up and running. Our advice, instructions, and recommendations are carefully and specifically tailored for a small network of two to eight computers. By focusing on small networks, rather than large and complicated operations, we eliminate a lot of complexity.

While you don't need to know anything about networks, we do assume that you know the basics about using your computers. (This would no longer be a little book if we tried to cover computer basics along with network basics!) If you're starting completely from square one—you don't know how to use a keyboard and mouse to edit text and to operate menus, windows, and other objects displayed on the computer screen—you need to learn how before beginning this book. To learn the basics

What You Should Already Know

of using a Windows PC, we recommend *The Little Windows 98 Book* by Alan Simpson (Peachpit Press, 1999). To learn the basics of using a Macintosh, we recommend *The Little Mac Book, 5th Edition*, by Robin Williams (Peachpit Press, 1998). When you know how to use your computers, return to this book to learn how to connect them in a network.

How to Use This Book The first part of this book explains why you should set up a network and how you do it. Start by reading Chapter 1 to get an overview of what your small network can do. Then read Chapter 2 to learn specifically what you'll need to connect your computers, and follow the chapter's detailed instructions to make the connections. Then follow the steps in Chapter 3 to set up each Windows PC and those in Chapter 4 to set up each Macintosh on your network.

By the time you finish the first part of the book, you should have your network ready to go and you should be ready to explore the second part of the book for details on what you can do with it: share an Internet connection, share printers, share files, play games, and more. In general, you don't have to read Chapters 5 through 9 consecutively. Take them in any order that makes sense for what you'd like to do on your network. One exception: read Chapter 7 before Chapter 8 to learn about sharing files.

The third part of this book contains reference information that you may find useful as you set up and use your network. Appendix A will help you troubleshoot problems, and a Glossary of networking terminology will help you understand networking technospeak.

Visual Cues As you read, look for the visual cues we've used to help you scan for information. **Headings** in the **outside margins** tell you the topic of the adjacent text. **Boldface** words in the text call your attention to key concepts and special network jargon. Speaking of jargon, we define all the terms you need to know right in the text as well as in the Glossary at the end of the book.

Icons in the margin point out tips, warnings, and notes.

Tip. This icon marks an idea or an alternative method that may make your networking life easier. A tip may also explain how to do something that is useful but somewhat unrelated to the topic under discussion.

Warning or caution. This icon denotes a description of a potential problem. If you don't heed warnings, your network may not work correctly or undesirable side effects may result. Beware of the dog!

Note. This icon draws your attention to noteworthy information about the subject under discussion. This is something you shouldn't miss, so pay close attention when you see this icon.

Part One
Network Nuts & Bolts

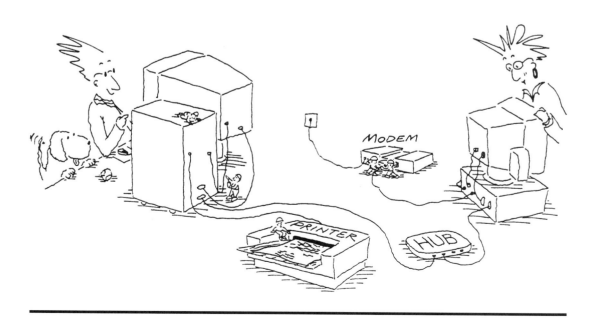

What Makes a Network Work?

Simply put, a **network** is some computers connected together so they can communicate with one another. A computer network is kind of like a telephone network—but far more capable. Of course, the telephone network is already set up for you by the phone company. Setting up a small computer network isn't quite as easy as plugging in telephones, but it's still pretty straightforward if you know what pieces you need (computers, modems, printers, etc.) and what to do with them. You're going to need some hardware for connecting these pieces, and you'll have to install some software. This chapter takes a look at the components of a network, the basics of installing one, and basic setup costs. But first let's explore what a network can do, so you'll know the advantages of having one of your own.

What a Network Can Do

When you think of a network, what comes first to mind? If you're like most people, you probably picture computers, printers, and lots of wires. However accurate this physical description may be, it misses what's important about a network—specifically, how it benefits you and other people in your home or small office. To get a picture of a network's benefits, imagine yourself taking part in these stories:

- Looking at your computer screen, you see an icon that represents a hard disk on a computer in the next room. You double-click the icon on your screen and see the other computer's files. You drag one of these files onto your computer's hard disk icon. Now you have a copy of this file. *This is a network.*

- You want to print some color illustrations for a report you're working on at home. Your computer is connected to a black-and-white laser printer, but your daughter's computer has a great color inkjet printer. No problem. You drag the illustration files to an icon on your screen that represents your daughter's printer. A few minutes later, in she walks, color illustrations in hand, saying "Hey, are these yours?" *This is a network.*

- You're playing a computer game, driving past your opponent, your friend Bob. You bragged to everyone that you could beat Bob, and now you're winning. Bob surprises you and cuts you off at the pass. *This is a network.*

- Bidding closes in five minutes on a must-have item being auctioned on the Internet. But you can keep downloading MP3 music on *your* computer while your dad makes a final bid from *his* computer, because your computers share an Internet connection. *This, too, is a network.*

*A network of computers in one location such as a home or small office is called a **local network**, also known as a **LAN** (local area network). Several local networks can be interconnected by long-distance links to form a **wide area network** (WAN).*

As you can see, a computer network lets people communicate on many different levels. When you think about it, using a network at home or in a small office opens almost endless possibilities: It would allow you to keep and update a family calendar or group schedule; to back up files from everyone's disks onto a shared tape drive; or to remotely control another computer as if you were in front of it. Later in this chapter, we'll look into even more ways to use a small network.

As you might expect, you'll get the benefits of using a network only if it has the necessary equipment. Naturally, you can't have a computer network without **computers** and the **hardware** that connects them. In addition, your network needs **software** to handle the **communications** between the connected computers. Let's take a closer look at all the gear that supports a network.

What a Network Needs

Some network know-it-all may tell you that you can make a network with one computer and a printer, and they'd be right. But they would also be missing the *point* of a network. To get network benefits like those described in the preceding section, you need **at least two** computers. You can of course have more than two computers on your network, but you need only two. The computers can be Windows PCs, Macs, or both.

At Least Two Computers

You may have heard that a network must have a powerful computer called a **server,** and that's usually true for medium-sized and large networks. In a small network, however, you don't need a server. We'll talk more about servers later in this chapter.

No server required

The **PCs** that you want to connect to your small network should have Windows 95 or Windows 98 installed. These versions of Windows are easiest to use and install in a small network.

Windows PCs

> **Avoid Using Older Versions of Windows.** You can also use PCs with Windows 3.1 and other previous versions in a network, although this book won't specifically tell you how. Configuring Windows 3.1 for networking can be considerably more difficult than configuring Windows 95 or 98. If you have an older PC with Windows 3.1 (or Windows for Workgroups), you should upgrade it to Windows 98 (or to Windows 95) before connecting it to a network.

> **Using Windows NT.** If you have a PC with Windows NT 4, you may be able to use it on your small network. You can follow most of the instructions in this book for Windows 95 and 98, because Windows NT 4 is outwardly similar to Windows 95.

> However, you'll have to resolve some differences on your own. For example, some Windows NT 4 dialog boxes have settings in different places than equivalent Windows 95 dialog boxes. You may also find that some of the products this book describes for Windows 95 and 98 do not work with Windows NT. In addition, Windows NT has advanced features for large networks that this book doesn't discuss.

Megahertz and Megabytes

Windows 95 and 98 require plenty of system resources—RAM, processor speed, and disk space—and connecting to a network does not diminish the requirements. For Windows 95, Microsoft says you can get by with 8MB of RAM and a 386 processor, but a more realistic minimum is 16MB of RAM and a 486 processor. Of course, any Intel Pentium processor or the equivalent from another manufacturer is great.

For Windows 98, Microsoft says 16MB of RAM is enough, but you really need at least 24MB for satisfactory operations. Since few PCs can have exactly 24MB, 32MB is the practical minimum. You also need a 66MHz 486DX2, a 100MHz 486DX4, or better processor. You may find performance sluggish with anything less than a 100MHz Pentium (or an equivalent from another manufacturer).

Macs

The **Macs** that you want to connect to your small network should be running System 7.5.5 or Mac OS 7.6 or later. You can also include a Mac that uses System 7.5.3, although upgrading it to System 7.5.5 is usually a good idea.

Using Older Mac Systems. It's possible to use old Macs with System 7.0.1–7.5.2 on a local network. You should, however, upgrade the old systems to use Open Transport, which is the Mac's second-generation networking software. This upgrade improves the performance and reliability of the old systems and gives them the networking control panels described in this book. If you include old Macs without Open Transport on your network, you'll have to figure out how to use their networking control panels on your own.

To use the second-generation Mac networking software described in this book, your Mac must have a 68030, 68040, or PowerPC processor. (PowerPC processors include the 601, 603, 604, G3 or 750, and G4.) You can connect an old Mac with a 68000 or 68020 processor to a network and share files and printers with it, but this book does not explain how to configure it for a network.

Network Hardware

The second most important physical part of a network is a means of connecting the computers. Traditionally, this has meant stringing wires around the house, as the phone company often does when you add a new phone line. You'll learn all about hooking up a network in the next chapter, but now let's take a quick look at what's involved.

For best performance and reliability, you'll want to wire your network with conventional **cables**. Network cables look a bit like thick phone cords, and their **connectors** look like overgrown phone cord connectors. Each computer in the network needs to have a network port that a

network cord can plug into. Your computer may already have a network port, but if it doesn't, you can easily add one (provided the computer has an unused expansion slot, of course).

New Wiring

If you're connecting only two computers, you can simply run a network cable from one to the other. With three or more networked computers, you run a network cable from each computer to a small central junction box called a **hub**.

RJ-45 Connector

Installing network cables is easier than you might expect. The degree of difficulty depends on the proximity of the computers in the network and how fussy you are about hiding the cables. If the computers are in the same room and you don't mind draping cables on the floor, ceiling, or walls, then installing network cables can be as easy as running speaker wires from a stereo system. (Because network cables don't carry enough electricity to shock you, do-it-yourself types can proceed fearlessly.)

What's harder is concealing network cables in walls, or connecting up computers that are located in separate rooms, especially if the rooms are not adjacent. In these situations, you may prefer to hire a network installer or a handyman who has the necessary skills.

If you don't like seeing or handling all those cables, you have other options for connecting your networked computers, *without* adding more wires.

Using Existing Wiring

It's now possible to connect computers in a network using existing **phone lines** or **power lines**. These types of networks, however, have a few drawbacks, as discussed in Chapter 2, "Connect the Computers." They can also be quite a bit slower than networks connected with conventional network wiring.

Wireless Connections

For even more freedom, you can use **wireless network adapters**. They transmit network data via radio signals that can pass through walls, floors, and ceilings up to a distance of about 150 feet, similar to those cordless phones that nearly everyone uses these days.

Like telephone-line and power-line networks, though, wireless networks suffer in the speed arena. Although a wireless network is fast enough for moderate activity on a small network, a conventional wired network is five to ten times faster. Also, wireless network software and installation isn't performing as well as it needs to be for widespread use. For more on wireless, including its drawbacks, see Chapter 2.

Why You Don't Need a Server

Often, a network found in a business environment will include a computer that's **dedicated** to providing a particular kind of data or service over the network. Like an electronic waiter, the **server** fulfills orders for data or services from anyone who uses the network. The server computer runs one or more specialized **server programs**. For instance, a **file server** program manages centralized file storage and file-sharing capabilities for everyone on the network. A **Web server** program serves up Web pages requested by Web browsers on the network.

To get the best performance out of a dedicated network server, its time is reserved for network work only. No one gets to use it for personal work or recreation.

Servers provide top performance when used in a large network, but your small network probably doesn't need a dedicated server. In a small network, rather than looking to a dedicated server, the computers look to each other for services. This arrangement is called a **peer-to-peer network**.

In peer-to-peer networks, computers communicate with each other without using a dedicated server. Each networked computer acts as a server to the others in the network. Some network services, such as file and printer sharing, are provided by Windows or the Mac OS without a server program running anywhere. Other services are provided by a server program running on one of the network computers. This server program can run in the background while someone actively uses the computer for another purpose, such as balancing a checkbook or browsing the Internet.

If you start your small network without a server, you can always add one later. In fact, you can turn any computer into a server simply by running server programs on it and not using it for anything else. You can even continue using peer-to-peer services such as file sharing *after* adding a server.

> For best performance and reliability, a dedicated server needs more robust network software than what you get with Windows 95, Windows 98, or Mac OS 8.6 and earlier. If you decide to add a dedicated server to your network at some point, you'll need to use heavy-duty software such as Windows NT, Linux, AppleShare IP, or Mac OS X Server on your server machine. This fact alone should cool any ardor you feel for a dedicated server.

Don't be confused or alarmed by network gurus who proclaim, "Every network must have a server!" This assertion may have been true in the past, but it's not true any more. A small network of computers running Windows 95, Windows 98, or Mac OS can do a lot without a dedicated server. Everything you'll learn about in this book can be done quite well with a peer-to-peer network—that is, without a server.

After you connect the computers in your network, the software running on them will establish communications over the network. This **network software** comes with your computer's operating system—be it Windows 95, Windows 98, or Mac OS. Before network communications can begin, you must set up the network software via some dialog boxes. You'll find instructions for setting up the network software in

Peer-to-Peer Networks

Dedicated network servers *aren't required for a small network, but they're a necessity for good performance in a large network.*

Network Software

Windows 95 and 98 in Chapter 3, "Set Up Your Windows Network Software"; instructions for Mac OS are in Chapter 4, "Set Up Your Mac Network Software."

Network Protocols

Setting up the network software enables the computers to communicate in a sort of language. In computer-speak, network languages are known as **protocols**. Several different protocols exist, and both Windows and Mac OS can use more than one simultaneously over the same network connections. For example, you might access a shared printer using one protocol while someone else accesses a shared Internet account using another protocol.

Each type of network service is generally designed to use a particular protocol. Some protocols are the same in Windows, Mac OS, and other operating systems. For example, Internet services use a common protocol. Other protocols are different for Windows PCs and Macs—the protocols for sharing files and printers, for instance.

Although every networked computer's system inherently supports a particular protocol or set of protocols, you can give your computer the ability to use foreign protocols by installing additional network software.

Ordinarily, you can use network services without having to think about these underlying protocols. But when you *add* network services, the protocols become very important. If your computer doesn't support the protocol required by a network service, for example, you won't be able to use the service. In later chapters, you'll learn about specific network services and the protocols they need, and how to make sure they're available on your computer.

The Illusion of Simultaneity

The network software on your computer and on another person's computer take split-second turns using the shared network. This happens so fast that you and other network users seem to have simultaneous use of the network.

Your Network's Services

Take network protocols and software, add network cables or other network connections, and you have the foundation of a network. But the reason you're going to all this trouble in the first place is to have a network that *does* something—in other words, it provides **network services**.

Sometimes you need extra hardware, too.

For each service you want your network to provide or access, you'll need more software. The software may be included with your computer, or you may have to add it. In addition, some network services also involve various pieces of equipment that must be connected to some computer on the network.

Let's go over some network services that your network can provide and see what each one needs. As you read, keep in mind that your network doesn't have to provide all these services. You can start with one network service and add more over time, as necessary.

You get some services "free" because they are included with the computer. For example, most Windows PCs and Macs come with preinstalled applications that can be used for browsing the World Wide Web (**browsers**) and exchanging **e-mail** on the Internet. Although you don't need a local network to use these applications on a computer with its own Internet connection, using a network enables several computers to share a single Internet connection simultaneously.

You'll need to acquire additional software or hardware to share an Internet account, as discussed in Chapter 5, "Share an Internet Connection."

Shared Internet Account

Your Windows PC or Mac also includes all the software you need to **share files and printers**. In fact, file and printer sharing are so thoroughly integrated into Windows and the Mac OS that you barely notice you're using a network. You simply drag and drop icons or choose menu commands just as you do when you work with files on your own disks and print to your own printer. Of course, these services must be set up properly to work over a network.

You'll learn how to configure your computer for printer and file sharing in Chapters 6 through 8.

Printer and File Sharing

In addition to those free network services, you can buy and install other application programs that provide other network services. These network-savvy applications are much like ordinary applications, except each one knows how to use the network to contact corresponding applications on other computers. For example, you can buy game programs designed for multiple players. The game program on each computer contacts its counterparts over the network to provide interactive play.

Chapter 9, "Serious Fun and Games," describes some of the multiplayer games you can use on a network.

Games for Multiple Players

> **Shop Smart.** When buying application programs for your networked computers, don't make the mistake of assuming that every application works over a network. Some applications come in both single-computer and networked-computer versions, and the network version may cost more. An application meant for networks usually includes a license for installing on a specific number of computers. Make sure the license allows you to install the application on all your computers, or at least on the ones that you want to have the network service that the application provides.

Messaging

Some application programs are available only for networks because they aren't useful on a single computer. For instance, **messaging programs** work like a private phone line between you and another person or persons using the network. You can send typed messages back and forth to carry on real-time "conversations." And if your computers include the necessary equipment, you can take this concept a step or two further. Microphones, for example, allow you to use your computer like a telephone, and a video camera lets you use your computer like a videophone.

Chapter 9 describes messaging services.

Group Calendar and Multiuser Database

In contrast to messaging programs, which work only if you have a network, are the applications that work without a network but have added dimensions with a network. These network-capable applications let you share information you previously kept for yourself, such as a list of names and addresses or a schedule of events and appointments. A personal address book and datebook can thus become part of a contact directory and calendar for a group. A collection of such information is called a **database**.

Using a network, you can share databases that include just about any type of information, so that each person using a network computer can both look up and change information while other people do the same. Chapter 9 also describes what you need to maintain a group calendar and contact directory, and to use a central database.

Networked File Backup

If you use your computer as most of us do—to store documents, data, spreadsheets, contacts, and other important information—you know how important it is to **back up your hard disk** on a regular basis. Otherwise, you risk losing important data in case of a computer malfunction, power outage, or other type of disaster. You can extend this backup function from the personal level to the network level.

- You may have used a backup program to copy files from your hard drive to Zip disks or to a tape drive that's connected to your computer. Your backup program may also be able to copy files from other computers over the network and store them on your tape drive.

- Or you can purchase a backup program that's designed to be used over a network. If you decide to purchase a new tape drive, many come equipped with a network backup program.

(Unfortunately, Zip disks don't hold enough information to be practical for network backup.)

- Still another approach is to have each networked computer use a shared Internet account to back up files onto rented space at an Internet site.

Chapter 9 has more information about what you need for network backups.

Using remote control software, you can actually use your mouse and keyboard to operate another computer on the network. With this software, you'll be able to see in a window on your own monitor what is being displayed on the other computer screen.

Remote Control Software

Chapter 9 also tells you about a couple of remote control programs you can get for computers running Windows and Mac OS .

It's probably clear to you by now that you'll need to spend some money to get the hardware and software required for setting up your network. Let's take a look at some ballpark numbers.

What a Network Costs

For starters, you may have to upgrade one or more of your computers to Windows 95 or 98; or if you use Macs, to System 7.5.5 or Mac OS 7.6.1 or later. Upgrading to the latest version of any of this software costs about $100. You might be able to find upgrades to one of the older versions for less.

Computer Upgrades

Upgrading to a newer operating system may require upgrading the computer's RAM and hard disk drive, as well. A RAM upgrade may cost $40 to $100, depending on the computer model. Be sure to shop around, since RAM prices vary a lot. A new hard drive costs $120 and up, depending on capacity. You may need to pay extra for installation and copying your old files to the new drive.

The cost for hardware that connects your computers will depend on the number of computers in your network, their proximity, and your choice of connection hardware.

Network Hardware

- For two computers in the same room, you can get by with $10 for a cable and $20 per computer for network adapter cards. You might not need a network adapter for a computer that already has a network port.

- If you have three or more computers and want to connect them with standard network cables, figure $10 per computer for cables and $20 per computer for network adapter cards. Again, you may not need a network adapter for a computer that already has a network port. Then add $30 for a hub that connects up to four computers, or $50 for an eight-computer hub. If the computers are located in different rooms, you'll have to spend more for longer cables, and you may want to hire someone to install the cables.

- If you're going to connect your computers without installing any new wiring, figure $50 to $100 per computer either for phone-line network adapters or power-line network adapters. Wireless network adapters run $100 to $150 per computer. All these adapters are complete and self-contained. You don't need to purchase any other hardware.

Network Software

As mentioned previously, basic network software is preinstalled on Windows PCs and Macs. You also get the necessary software to provide some network services, such as file and printer sharing. For other services, you'll have to buy additional software and, in some cases, hardware. These costs vary widely depending on what products you decide to buy.

How to Make a Network

Now that you've read about the benefits of a network, learned what hardware and software it takes to set up a network, and formed a rough idea of the cost, you're ready to begin putting together your own network. Here's what you have to do:

1. Choose a type of network.
2. Connect the network hardware.
3. Set up the network software.
4. Add network services.

The rest of this book takes you through these steps in order. So roll up your sleeves, and let's get going!

Summary

A computer network, like a telephone network, enables communications. But unlike a telephone network, these communications can include sharing documents, database files, Internet access, and more. A computer becomes a more useful and powerful tool when it can communicate with and access other computers, and the advantages of a network will repay the cost and effort it takes to set one up.

▼ A network can provide many benefits to you and other people who use computers in your home or small office, such as **sharing an Internet account, printers, data, and files**.

▼ To get the benefits of a network, you need to connect **at least two computers**. They can be Windows PCs, Macs, or both.

▼ Cables, connector boxes, adapter cards, and related hardware are the most common means of **connecting network computers**, but you can set up a wireless network or a network that uses phone or power-line wiring that's already in place.

▼ The **network software** included with Windows and Mac OS enables your computers to communicate using network languages called **protocols**.

▼ The software that provides some network services, including printer sharing and file sharing, is **included with Windows and Mac OS software**.

▼ You can add network services one at a time by obtaining more software and, in some cases, hardware. **Additional services** include Internet account sharing, multiplayer gaming, chatting, sharing a group calendar or multiuser database file, file backup, file synchronization, and remote access to another computer.

▼ The **cost** of a network may include the cost of upgrading to a newer version of Windows or Mac OS and improving RAM and hard disk drives. Networking costs also include cables, network adapter cards, and hubs, or adapters for phone-line, power-line, or wireless networks.

Connect the Computers

Computers can't communicate by shouting across the room. They need to be connected in a network, and that's your job. You may also need to install some hardware to make those computers ready to be connected to their network, and you may need to run some wires. But relax— although these tasks may sound daunting, they're easy enough if you take it a step at a time. Your first step is to decide what type of network you want to install.

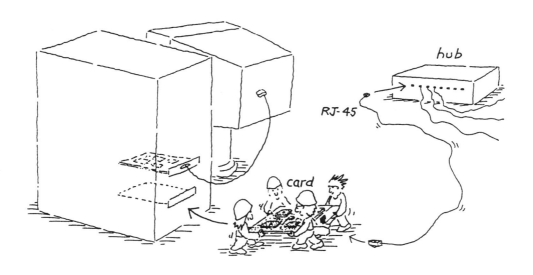

Choose a Type of Network

Connecting two or three computers in the same room is a simple matter; you can plug in a few cables and have a network in a few minutes. For a larger groups of computers, however, or for computers located in different rooms, you had better think about what you are installing and where. When more than three computers are involved and the distance between them is greater, you need to do some planning.

Several types of network hardware are appropriate for a small network: Ethernet, Fast Ethernet, and LocalTalk are well established. Newer, although problematic, alternatives include phone-line, power-line, and wireless. Let's see how these networks stack up in terms of performance, ease of installation, and compatibility.

Ethernet Networks

The most common network hardware system for PCs and Macs is **Ethernet**. Ethernet hardware works with all the popular Windows and Mac OS network protocols, or languages, including TCP/IP, NetBEUI, IPX/SPX, and AppleTalk. If what you want to do can be done on a network, you can do it on Ethernet; that's one reason why more networks use Ethernet hardware than any other kind.

*Ethernet's speed, reliability, and security make it the **best choice for most small networks**.*

In addition to working with many protocols, Ethernet scales well from very small networks to very large networks. Several types of Ethernet equipment are available in different price ranges, offering various performance levels. Some suit large networks best, and others are just the ticket for small networks.

The cheapest and most popular type of Ethernet hardware is called **10BaseT**. The 10 stands for **10 megabits per second (Mbps)**, which is the maximum speed at which data can move over the network.

A Network that Grows: A 10BaseT network isn't just for small networks. Although your network will probably include only a few computers and perhaps a printer or a cable modem, you can connect more than 200 computers and other devices in a single 10BaseT network.

Ethernet Speed

Ethernet is fast. A Web page that would take a minute to download on a 56K modem takes as little as a few seconds to transfer on a 10BaseT network. Because 10BaseT is fast and affordable, and it works on both PCs and Macs, it is the most popular type of small network.

Ethernet Wiring

As you may have gathered from all this talk of Ethernet hardware, setting up a 10BaseT network means installing new wiring—but at least the wiring is relatively inexpensive and easy to work with. The **10BaseT**

cables resemble large phone cords; even the connectors look like overgrown modular phone connectors.

Using these cables, you connect each computer or other network device to a **10BaseT hub** (a central junction box). If you need to connect only two computers, you can omit the hub and simply connect the computers to each other with a specially wired 10BaseT cable (more about this later).

In addition to a network cable, each computer on an Ethernet must have a 10BaseT **Ethernet port**. Some computers, especially newer Macs, have a built in Ethernet port. You'll find the Ethernet port on the back or side of the computer, where the printer, mouse, and keyboard ports are located. If you don't see one on your computer, you can install a 10BaseT **network adapter card**. These adapter cards are available for desktop PCs that have PCI or ISA expansions slots (most PCs have these), for notebook computers with PC card slots, for desktop Macs with a variety of expansion slots, and for Macintosh PowerBooks (Apple's notebook computers) with PC card slots.

*A **port** is a connection point.*

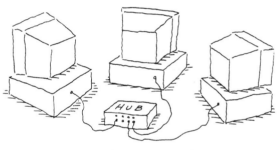

10BaseT Ethernet

The 10BaseT cables connecting your computers with other devices in the network can extend up to 328 feet (100 meters) from the 10BaseT hub. Do the math, and you'll see that this means your computers and other equipment can have as much as 650 feet (200 meters) of cable strung between them and still work.

Ethernet Range

Keep in mind that these distances refer to the length of the network wires, which may *not* be the shortest distance between computers. Network wires usually run alongside or inside walls, not straight across rooms. You could have as much as 650 feet of wire coiled up on the floor between two computers resting side-by-side, but we wouldn't recommend that!

Fast Ethernet Networks

If you think you'll be moving a lot of data over your network, such as video, music, or large graphics, you might consider spending a little more money to install **Fast Ethernet**. Also known as **100BaseT**, Fast Ethernet transmits data over the network at a maximum rate of 100Mbps. In theory, that's ten times faster than 10BaseT—but network speed is affected by many factors that limit the actual rate of transmission. 100BaseT in practice is usually less than seven times faster than 10BaseT.

100BaseT has other advantages over 10BaseT that don't apply to small networks, such as the ability to accommodate more computers without bogging down. Like 10BaseT networks, 100BaseT networks work with both PCs and Macs.

Higher Cost; More Speed

A 100BaseT network looks almost identical to a 10BaseT network, and setup is identical. 100BaseT requires a higher grade of cables and connectors, and the hubs and adapter cards are designed to operate at higher speeds. These differences make 100BaseT network hardware cost more than 10BaseT, although prices are falling. 100BaseT hardware may eventually become affordable enough to be the preferred choice over 10BaseT.

Outpacing even 100BaseT Ethernet, **Gigabit Ethernet** *is faster than most small networks need.*

You can mix 100BaseT and 10BaseT on the same network. Most 100BaseT hardware—adapter cards, built-in Ethernet ports, and hubs—is actually **10/100BaseT** hardware, which automatically determines whether to operate at 10Mbps or 100Mbps. (Even Apple's little iMac has a 10/100BaseT port built in.) A 10/100BaseT adapter senses whether it's connected to a 10BaseT hub or a 100BaseT hub and then operates at the appropriate rate. Likewise, a 10/100BaseT hub senses the best rate to use for each computer connected to the hub. This auto-sensing 10/100BaseT hardware makes it very easy to upgrade the network from 10BaseT to 100BaseT gradually, one machine at a time, rather than all at once.

LocalTalk Networks

If you are connecting only a few older Macs, you might consider using LocalTalk. It's quite a bit slower than Ethernet, but it's also a lot cheaper and easier to set up on older machines. LocalTalk's maximum rate is 230.4 kilobytes per second (Kbps), or 0.225Mbps. Although 10BaseT is theoretically more than 40 times faster, tests show it is actually about 5 times faster than LocalTalk on a small network. That's plenty fast enough for sharing a printer, some files, and an Internet connection among several Macs.

LocalTalk and AppleTalk: LocalTalk was called AppleTalk before Ethernet came to the Mac. Now LocalTalk means the cables and other network hardware that connect to Mac serial ports (such as the printer port); and AppleTalk is the Apple network protocol. The LocalTalk hardware always uses the AppleTalk protocol, but the AppleTalk protocol itself can also be used with other network hardware such as Ethernet.

Macs without LocalTalk: The iMac, the 1999 Power Mac G3, and the 1999 PowerBook G3 don't have a port for a LocalTalk connector. LocalTalk is nearing the end of its useful life, thanks to falling prices on 10BaseT Ethernet hardware. Don't be surprised if Apple forgoes LocalTalk on all new Mac models.

You don't need LocalTalk network adapters because every Macintosh except the newest models has a built-in port where you can plug in a LocalTalk connector. Most Apple LaserWriter printers and some other Mac printers also have LocalTalk ports. You don't need a hub; you simply connect one Mac to another in a **daisy chain** configuration (shown below). You can hook up a LocalTalk network with ordinary telephone cords like the ones you use to plug a phone into a phone jack. In fact, if you have only one phone line in your house or office, you can probably extend a LocalTalk network from room to room by plugging into existing wall jacks. Most in-wall telephone cables have two pairs of wires: Your telephone uses one pair, and LocalTalk can probably use the other pair.

Daisy Chain

PCs with LocalTalk: Although LocalTalk adapters are available for PCs, you're better off using Ethernet hardware all around.

Alternative Network Types

Along about now you may be thinking, "As much as I'd like to network my computers, I can't bear the thought of all that new wiring." The good news is that there are several alternative types of networks that don't require new wiring. Instead, they transmit network data via existing telephone wiring, existing electrical wiring, or radio signals. Compared to Ethernet, these alternative networks are very easy to install.

The bad news is that the alternative networks don't work well for everyone. At their best, they are all slower than Ethernet. At their worst, computers on these networks may be unable to contact each other or may have trouble staying in contact. In addition, all these alternative networks are less secure than Ethernet.

Phone-line, power-line, and wireless alternatives are expected to improve over time. We won't spend a lot of time explaining their every nuance, but following are brief descriptions.

Phone-Line Networks

If you want to avoid the hassle of installing new wiring, you might be able to use your existing telephone wiring for a computer network. In a phone-line network, cables connect to your computers via an internal or external phone-line adapter, and the computers plug into the same kind of phone-line jacks as those used by your telephones, answering machine, and modem.

This network uses the same pair of wires used by the regular telephone equipment, setting the phone-line network apart from the LocalTalk network described earlier. LocalTalk can use an alternate pair of wires that are part of the same cable as the pair used by the regular telephone equipment and a phone-line network.

Peaceful Coexistence

Although the phone-line network uses the same wiring used by your phone, fax, and modem, there's no confusion across the wires because a phone-line network sends its signals at a different frequency than regular telephone equipment.

Phone Line

Phone-line networks use the same network protocols as Ethernet, including TCP/IP, NetBEUI, IPX/SPX, and AppleTalk. If a network service works on an Ethernet network, it will probably work on a phone-line network as well.

Range

The phone-line network signal maintains its speed and strength over about 500 feet of phone wire, putting the maximum distance between two networked computers in the same ballpark as a 10BaseT or 100BaseT Ethernet network. (Like Ethernet wiring, phone wiring seldom follows a straight path; and the direct distance between computers will be less than the length of the wire between them.)

Phone-line networks might sound like the easiest way to go, but it's not so simple. Yes, they're easier to hook up than Ethernet networks if you have computers in several rooms. But phone-line networks are slower than 10BaseT Ethernet (and a *lot* slower than 100BaseT Ethernet). A phone-line network transfers data at up to 1Mbps. Sharing a couple of printers won't tax a phone-line network, and neither will sharing files that are no more than a few megabytes each. Phone-line networks are also fast enough for two or three computers to browse most Web pages on the Internet via a shared connection. You'll notice a performance difference if you try to copy large files between computers or view high-resolution streaming video via a cable modem or DSL connection to the Internet.

Drawbacks

Security considerations can also come into play. Part of the 500 feet traveled by network signals may extend outside your home or office. Your phone wiring keeps going beyond your exterior walls, and the network signal can go right along with it.

> Phone-line networks have not been time-tested as Ethernet has. The technology and products are new, relatively speaking, so you may encounter kinks that take time to work out. When we wrote this book in early 1999, phone-line networks worked for many people but not for everyone.

**Power-Line
Networks**

Electrical power lines can be used even more effectively than a phone-line network to avoid installing new wiring. Your computers connect to the network, via adapters, by plugging into electrical wall outlets. Adapters are available for PCs and network printers with parallel port connectors. (These adapters don't work with Macs, because Macs don't have parallel port connectors at all.)

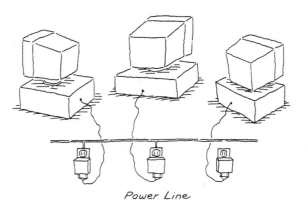

Power Line

Drawbacks

As it is with other alternatives to Ethernet, speed is a concern on a power-line network. A power-line network has a top rate of 350Kbps—slower than a phone-line network, and much slower than a 10BaseT Ethernet network, but still faster than a 56K modem.

Security is also an issue with a power-line network. The network signals can travel up to a quarter-mile outside your house or office, but not past the power line transformer that feeds power to your house or office. So neighbors who share your transformer can get your network signals if they're using a compatible power-line network (which, let's face it, isn't likely). If you don't want a public network, you can keep it private by turning on encryption. However, encryption slows network performance.

Unlike Ethernet, the technology behind power-line networks is not a widely accepted standard. Some people are able to get power-line networks working reliably with little effort, but others have no such luck. Plus, there's no telling how long phone-line products will be around. You might go ahead and try this alternative type of network, but don't be surprised if you end up using Ethernet.

Power-line and phone-line networks alleviate most of the burden of physically wiring a network, but they still leave your computers tethered to a nearby jack or outlet. Wireless networks, in contrast, are truly untethered. These networks use radio waves to transmit signals from a wireless network adapter that combines the function of a regular network adapter with a radio transmitter and receiver. You can find adapter cards for desktop PCs with ISA or PCI expansion slots, PC cards for notebook computers, and external adapter boxes that plug into a PC's parallel or USB connector. None of the wireless network adapters made for the home and small office market will work with Macs.

Wireless Networks

Wireless

Computers on a wireless network can't be positioned as far apart as they can on other types of networks. The maximum range of wireless network adapters is 150 feet, and that's in open air. The radio signals can pass through most walls, floors, and ceilings, but thick concrete, brick, and metal will block the radio signals.

Drawbacks

Wireless networks made for home and small offices are slower than Ethernet. Some wireless networks operate at the same rate as phone-line networks (1Mbps); others are rated at 0.5 or 1.6 Mbps. Speed decreases under adverse conditions, such as operating near the range limit.

Security is another concern with anything that broadcasts radio signals. However, wireless network adapters prevent eavesdropping on your network by switching the radio frequency (channel) many times every second, so a neighbor who uses the same brand of network can't tap into yours.

> Wireless home networks, like other alternatives to Ethernet, are easy to hook up but can be difficult to get working. And, like the other non-Ethernet alternatives, it's difficult to speculate the wireless network's future. You may have better luck with one brand of home wireless-network products than another, but they're all still a far cry from Ethernet.

Planning and Installing an Ethernet Network

Even though Ethernet is the most efficient type of small network, you have to be ready for it. You have to think about how you're going to run the wires. You also have to make sure every computer has an Ethernet port, which may involve installing adapter cards.

In this section, we'll tell you about how to plan for what you'll need to hook up an Ethernet network. We'll discuss all the necessary equipment, including network adapters and wiring; and we'll tell you how to install this equipment.

Planning the Wiring

Before installing your network, give some thought to the physical layout for the wiring—where you're going to put it and whether you want it hidden or not. Also, decide whether you want to do it yourself or hire an expert.

> To help plan the network wiring, make a rough drawing of your home or office floor plan. Mark where you think the computers, the hub, and the cables will go, to give you an idea of how much cable to buy.

The Hub

Most Ethernet networks require a hub, and its location can affect how much wiring you need to install. (We'll give you advice on buying hubs in the upcoming section "Choosing a Hub.")

> If you have two computers located close to each other, you can connect them without a hub and without planning any wiring. Instead, you'll connect the computers with a specially wired cable called a **crossover cable**. (You'll find the details in the section "Cables and Jacks," later in this chapter.)

You'll want to locate your hub centrally. A central location can minimize the amount of cable you need and keep costs down. A central location also minimizes the chance that you'll need more than the maximum 328 feet of cable allowed between the hub and any computer. Make sure the location you pick for your hub has a nearby electrical outlet, because most hubs must be plugged in.

- In an office, the hub usually goes inside a utility closet.
- At home, you'll probably use a small hub that can go next to your desk or on a shelf, or it can just hang off the back of one of the computers (some hubs are no bigger than a mouse).

Network wiring is safe in a home environment because it doesn't carry a voltage that could harm you, your kids, or your pets. It carries signals about as strong as those in a telephone wire, so you can run a network wire under a carpet without creating a fire hazard. Keep in mind, though, that if a lot of traffic crosses that carpet, the cable underneath could eventually be damaged and need replacement. You can also run network cable along the wall or baseboard at the floor, stapling or nailing with special hooked nails every few feet.

For a more finished look, you can route cables through surface raceway—a metal or plastic channel with a removable cover. Remove the cover and attach the channel to the wall or baseboard; then lay the cable in the channel and snap the cover over it. Simple!

If you need to route a cable across the floor where someone might walk near or on it, install a cord cover over it. Cord covers are ramped on both edges so people won't trip over them, and the cable is held steady in a channel along the bottom. Office supply and hardware stores carry cord covers made for electrical extension cords, and they'll work for network cables as well.

> If you need to bend the cables, the turns should be smooth, with at least a 2-inch radius. Don't kink cables or bend them sharply, or they may transmit network signals slowly and unreliably. These rules are especially important for 100BaseT networks, which are more susceptible to interference than 10BaseT.

To avoid unsightly draping, creeping, or under-rug cables in your home or office, you can install cables inside walls, under floors, and above ceilings. However, this can be the most expensive part of installing a network. And hiring a contractor to do the job can cost hundreds of dollars.

If you're a do-it-yourselfer, pick up a book on basic home electrical wiring and read it—*before* you start drilling holes. Network cables are much more flexible than electrical wires, so fishing network cables through small drilled holes should be easier than threading electrical wiring.

Exposed Wiring

Be careful to staple or nail over the cable, never through it!

Concealed Wiring

Your networking area may be on a top floor with an attic above, or you may have a **suspended ceiling** (the kind with large acoustic tiles that you can push up from below). In these situations, you can run the cable up into the attic or ceiling, horizontally through the attic or across ceiling tiles, and then down into another room.

Watch Out for Lighting Fixtures: If you're running cables above a suspended ceiling, you must give a wide berth to florescent lights and the electrical wires that feed them. These fixtures can cause electromagnetic interference that slows or disrupts network flow. To be safe, keep network cables at least 3 feet away from electrical wires and fluorescent lights.

About PVC Cable: Network cables are available with two types of insulation. There's no denying cables with PVC (polyvinyl chloride) are inexpensive—but in the event of a fire they will release a poisonous gas. Building codes prohibit installing PVC cable above a building's suspended ceiling that is part of the building's ventilation system (called the plenum air return). Cables installed in this space must have plenum-grade insulation, such as Teflon.

If your network is on the ground floor with a basement or crawl space below, you can run the cable below the floor. Then run the cable horizontally beneath the floor and bring it up in another room.

Other Suggestions for Concealed Wiring

When you don't want the cables to be exposed but you aren't too excited by the prospect of fishing them through the wall, ceiling, or floor, you can route the wiring behind the baseboard of floors and the molding of doorways. Be careful removing the molding, especially if you want to keep and re-attach the same wood; it breaks easily.

After you make wiring and layout plans for your network, you should acquire all the network hardware you'll need. That way you'll have everything on hand right when you need it, and more importantly, you'll get a chance to become familiar with the pieces and how you'll integrate them.

Getting the Hardware

Here's a short list of the hardware you'll need to set up an Ethernet network, followed by descriptions of each item:

- An Ethernet adapter card for each computer that doesn't have an Ethernet port
- A transceiver for each Mac with an AAUI Ethernet port
- A hub if you're connecting more than two computers
- Cables and possibly wall jacks

Every computer needs an Ethernet port. In some computers, the Ethernet port is built into the motherboard (the computer's main circuit board). Other machines require an Ethernet adapter card. If you'll be setting up a standard 10Mbps Ethernet network, every computer must have a 10BaseT or 10/100BaseT port. If you opt for a fast 100Mbps Ethernet network, every computer must have a 10/100BaseT port.

Ethernet Connectors

If you buy a new Ethernet adapter card, you'll most likely pick up a 10/100BaseT adapter. A straight 100BaseT adapter is an older design that was used chiefly in high-speed corporate networks and is not common these days. However, in a fast Ethernet network, straight 100BaseT will work as well as dual-speed 10/100BaseT.

10/100BaseT vs. 100BaseT Adapters

Existing Ethernet Connectors

Some of your computers may already have the required Ethernet port installed, some may have the wrong kind of Ethernet port, and some may have no Ethernet port at all. Take a look at the back or side of each computer. If it's ready for Ethernet, you'll see an **RJ-45 jack**, which looks like a phone or modem jack but is larger. Watch out—don't mistake the small RJ-11 modem jack for the larger RJ-45 Ethernet jack!

The computer may have another kind of Ethernet connection point, such as a 15-pin D-shaped AUI (Attachment Unit Interface) or a bayonet-style BNC (British Naval Connector). Usually these connection points exist alongside an RJ-45 jack; you can simply ignore these extra connection points.

Recognizing 10/100BaseT Ports

You can't tell by looking at an RJ-45 jack whether it's for a 10BaseT port or a 10/100BaseT port —both types of Ethernet use an RJ-45 jack. If you're installing a 10BaseT network, a 10BaseT or 10/100BaseT port will do. However, if you're installing a 100BaseT Fast Ethernet network, a 10BaseT port won't fill the bill. On some computers, near the RJ-45 jack you'll see an LED labeled "100," which tells you that you have a 10/100BaseT port. You can also check the computer's specifications to determine the type of Ethernet it has. If all else fails, you can proceed on the assumption that the computer has a 10/100BaseT port; should it later turn out that this computer doesn't show up on your Fast Ethernet network, you can install a 10/100BaseT adapter card at that time.

Transceivers for Macintosh AAUI Ports

If you're using an older Mac that lacks an RJ-45 jack, it may nevertheless have a usable Ethernet port. Many older Macintosh models have a general-purpose Ethernet port called **AAUI** (Apple Attachment Unit Interface). You can convert an AAUI port to a 10BaseT port by attaching a small box, called a **transceiver**, to it.

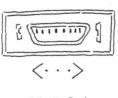

AAUI Port

You'll need an Ethernet adapter for each computer that has the wrong kind of Ethernet ports or no Ethernet ports at all.

- The most common adapters for desktop PCs are internal cards for PCI or ISA slots (also known as **NICs**, or Network Interface Cards). Notebook computers often use PC card adapters (also known as PCMCIA card), although some have special internal adapters.

- For desktop Macs without a built-in Ethernet port, adapter cards are available for all the different expansion slots in various Macintosh models, including Communications (Comm), NuBus, and PDS slots. You can also get a PCI or NuBus adapter to upgrade a Macintosh with a built-in Ethernet port to 10/100BaseT, although NuBus adapters have to operate at less than 100Mbps because NuBus slots are too slow.

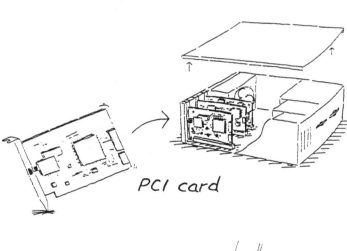

PCI card

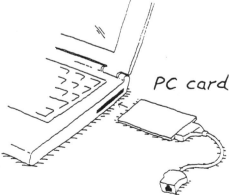

PC card

Plan Ahead for 100BaseT: Even if you don't need the speed of 100BaseT today, you should go ahead and get a 10/100BaseT adapter for each computer that doesn't already have a 10BaseT connector. The 10/100's don't cost much more than straight 10BaseT adapters, yet they work at 10Mbps in a 10BaseT network today and will automatically switch themselves to 100Mbps when you upgrade to a 100BaseT network. (To upgrade, you need a hub and wiring that are compatible with 100BaseT, as discussed later in "Installing Hubs" and "Cables and Jacks.")

Adapter Issues
for PCs

When buying an Ethernet adapter card for a desktop PC, **make sure the card matches an unused slot** in the computer—that is, get an ISA card for an ISA slot or a PCI card for a PCI slot.

If you're installing a 10BaseT network and the computer has both kinds of slots available, you can use either kind of card. Note, however, that PCI cards have a couple of advantages on some PCs. If the PC is running Windows 98, or Windows 95 OSR2.0 or 2.1, a PCI adapter won't conflict with other parts of the PC, where an ISA adapter could. In addition, a PCI card is also better for a 10/100BaseT adapter because an ISA slot is actually slower than a 100BaseT network.

Make sure a PCI or ISA adapter card complies with the Windows Plug and Play feature. **Plug and Play** enables Windows 95 and 98 to recognize the card and automatically install the necessary driver software. The Plug and Play feature is not available in any version prior to Windows 95 (that is, any of the Windows 3.x versions). Installing an Ethernet adapter in Windows 3.x can be a real headache, and you can spend hours trying to configure settings that are automatically configured for you in Windows 95 and 98. This is one of the reasons why you need to upgrade all your PCs to Windows 95 or 98 before connecting them to your network.

Adapter Issues
for Macs

Macs don't need
Plug and Play cards.

If you're after an internal Ethernet adapter for a Macintosh, be sure to specify the Macintosh model before you buy. The various Mac models use different kinds of internal expansion slots, and you need an adapter that fits the kind of slot present in your Mac. If your Mac has PCI slots, get a PCI card that's made for Macs or for Macs and PCs. If you get a PCI card made only for PCs, it probably won't work on a Mac.

As mentioned, if you have more than two devices to connect to your Ethernet network, you need a **hub**. A hub is just a box with a bunch of RJ-45 jacks and lights that flash to indicate network activity. Its purpose is to propagate the signal from any one of the network computers to all of the other network computers.

Choosing a Hub

> Although you don't have to use a hub with only two computers, you certainly may. In fact, if one or more of your computers is a Mac, a hub will simplify your daily life (as you'll see later in this chapter).

Hubs can have 4 or 5 ports, 8 ports, 12 ports, 16 ports, or even more. Make sure you get a hub with enough ports for all your computers, network printers, and other network devices, plus a few spare ports for the computers you might want to add later.

Every computer, network printer, network modem, and other connected device plugs directly into the hub.

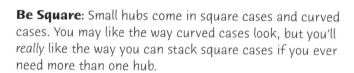

8-Port Hub

4-Port Hub

> **Be Square:** Small hubs come in square cases and curved cases. You may like the way curved cases look, but you'll *really* like the way you can stack square cases if you ever need more than one hub.

If you get a great deal on a five-port hub that works for now, but you anticipate needing more ports later on when you add computers, don't worry about it—you can add ports by getting another hub and linking it to the existing hub. You link hubs by running a regular Ethernet cable from the specially marked uplink port of one hub to any ordinary port of the other hub. If neither hub has an uplink port, you can link the hubs by connecting the ordinary ports of the units with a crossover cable. (The story on cables is coming up.)

Linking Hubs

Although you're not likely to link more than two or three hubs in a small network, be aware that there is a limit on hub linking. Your network can't have more than three hubs on the path between any two computers or other network devices. This restriction is sometimes called the **four-hop rule**: Each length of cable between two computers is known as a **hop**. Count the number of hops between two computers that have three hubs between them, and you'll count four hops—the maximum.

Types of Hubs

The speed rating of the hub you use must match the speed rating of your computer's Ethernet connectors. The table below summarizes your options. A 10/100BaseT hub is the most flexible because it works with all the Ethernet connectors you're likely to use in your small network—10BaseT, 10/100BaseT, and 100BaseT. A plain 10BaseT hub costs the least and will work with all connectors except straight 100BaseT. Of course, the dual-speed hub performs better than the 10BaseT hub on computers with 10/100BaseT connectors.

Connectors in the Network	Type of Hub 10BaseT	10/100BaseT	100BaseT
10BaseT only	Best	OK	No
10BaseT and 10/100BaseT	OK	Best	No
10/100BaseT only	OK	Best	OK
10BaseT and 100BaseT	No	Best	No
10/100BaseT and 100BaseT	No	Best	OK
100BaseT only	No	Best	OK
10BaseT, 10/100BaseT, and 100BaseT	No	Best	No

Upgrading to 100BaseT: There's no need to buy a 10/100BaseT hub now just because you think you might want a 100BaseT network someday. When you're ready for a faster network, you can replace your 10BaseT hub with a 10/100BaseT hub, as long as you have the higher-quality cables that 100BaseT requires (more about these cables coming up in the next section). Or link your old 10BaseT hub to a new 10/100BaseT hub; then use the slower hub for computers with 10BaseT, and the faster hub for computers with 10/100BaseT.

On the outside, 10BaseT and 100BaseT Ethernet cables look like phone cables, but on the inside are at least two pairs of twisted wire, appropriately known as **twisted pair**. The twisting of the wires shields them against electrical interference from external sources; the more twisting, the less susceptible the wires are to interference. Twisted-pair cables are available with or without additional internal shielding, but 10BaseT and 100BaseT use the kind without extra shielding, which is sometimes called **unshielded twisted pair (UTP)**.

Cables and Jacks

The **T** in 10BaseT and 100BaseT stands for **twisted pair**.

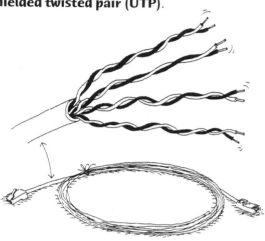

RJ-45 Twisted Pair Cable

Twisted-pair cables have RJ-45 plugs at the ends, which mate with the jacks used for the 10BaseT and 100BaseT Ethernet ports. Cables with RJ-45 plugs at both ends are sometimes called **patch cables**.

RJ-45 Plugs

You can buy preassembled, fully tested cables in various lengths and colors, or you can buy cable and plugs in bulk and assemble them yourself. The preassembled cables are your best bet unless you're running cable through walls, floors, or closed ceilings, in which case you'll probably need to work with bulk cable.

Bulk and Preassembled Cables

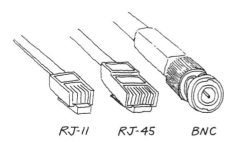

RJ-11   RJ-45   BNC

Do-It-Yourselfers Beware: You might think you're saving money by making your own cables, because the bulk parts cost less than the preassembled cables. However, you have to buy a special crimping tool to attach the plugs to the cable and then take the time to assemble the cables. Furthermore, there's always the oh-so-remote possibility that you may goof up a cable by getting the wires in the wrong order or untwisting too much wire at the end of the cable. Hey, accidents happen!

Jacks

If you're running bulk cable between computers and the hub, you'll need an **RJ-45 jack** at each computer location and at the location of any other network devices—such as cable modems or printers—that connect directly to the network (not to a computer on the network). You run a length of bulk cable from each jack to the vicinity of your hub. Where all the cables come together near the hub, you connect each one to another jack. It's a good idea to label each jack near the hub so you know where it leads. (Later, you'll connect each of these jacks to the hub.)

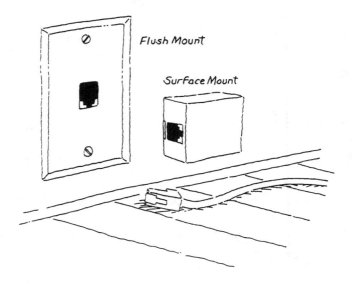

Jacks provide a professional touch.

You won't need jacks and bulk cable if you can safely and conveniently route preassembled cables from the hub to every computer. However, if you need to run cables through floors, ceilings, and walls, you should use bulk cable and attach each end to a jack. If you try to run preassembled cables through holes in the wall or floor, you'll have to drill much bigger holes and you may damage the plug as you push and pull it through the hole.

In addition, jacks save wear and tear on your permanently installed cables. If the patch cable between the jack and the computer gets damaged at some point, you can easily replace it. If you don't use a jack, however, and the permanent cable gets damaged between the wall and the computer, you have to splice the cable or replace it. What's more, jacks look neater than lengths of cable flopping out of the wall.

When you shop for twisted-pair cables, plugs, and jacks, you'll find several grades labeled by category numbers. The higher the category, the better the quality and the more the item costs. For 10BaseT, you can use a **category 3** or higher. For 100BaseT, however, you need **category 5**. Follow these rules not only for cables but for any RJ-45 plugs, jacks, or patch panels that you buy separately.

Category 3 or 5 Cables

> **Consider Category 5 Cables**: If you are spending the money to install cables inside walls, floors, or ceilings, you should go with category 5 cables and jacks in case you later decide to upgrade your network to 100BaseT. You'll pay a little more now, but you'll avoid expensive rewiring later. And the superior wiring works just fine for a 10BaseT network.
>
> When you're shopping for cables, you'll sound like a pro if you ask for "cat 5" or "cat 3" cables instead of "category 5" or "category 3."

If your network will have only two computers, and you're planning to connect them in a 10BaseT network without a hub, you need a special cable called a **crossover cable**. The wires in this type of cable are crossed in one of the plugs.

Crossover Cable

In a regular 10BaseT cable, the wires are arranged in exactly the same order in both plugs, but in a crossover cable, the two wires of each pair are reversed in one plug. This is necessary because one wire of each pair is for sending network signals and the other wire of each pair is for receiving. By crossing the send and receive wires at one end of the plug, you make each computer send signals on the wire that the other computer uses to receive signals. If the wires weren't crossed, it would be like someone trying to use the telephone with the handset upside down. You don't connect computers to a hub with crossover cables because it keeps the send and receive wires in order.

You can obtain a crossover cable from most sources of regular cables.

Attention Mac Users: Macs don't particularly like crossover cables. If you use these cables, when both of your networked Macs are off and you turn one on, it will complain that it can't use Ethernet and will reset the AppleTalk control panel to use the Printer port instead. After you turn on the second computer, you have to reset the first computer's AppleTalk control panel to Ethernet.

Starter Kits

You can buy Ethernet adapters, cables, and hubs individually, or you can buy a starter kit that includes enough of these items to connect two computers. Generally, the starter kits are a good value, even if you have to supplement them with Ethernet adapters and cables for additional computers. At the very least, everything you need to get a small network started is already gathered in one place.

Cable Exotica

You may have heard about other kinds of Ethernet cable (such as **thinnet**, **thicknet**, or **fiber optic**), but you don't need to consider using them for a small network. Twisted pair cable is easier to handle and costs less than the other options, whose main advantages are less susceptibility to magnetic and electrical interference and the ability to span greater distances than twisted pair.

Installing Network Adapters

After you have obtained all the equipment you need to connect your computers, you're ready to install it. First, you install the network adapters you got for your computers that don't already have network ports.

PC Cards for Notebooks

Installing a PC card network adapter in a notebook computer is easy because you don't even have to open the computer.

To install a PC card:

1. Shut down the notebook computer. (This step may not be necessary with all notebooks, but it can't hurt.)

2. Slide the card into the notebook's PC card slot and press the card firmly into place.

3. Turn on the computer and install the software included with the card.

In addition, you need to set up the network software on the computer. We cover these procedures in Chapter 3, "Set Up Your Windows Network Software," and Chapter 4, "Set Up Your Mac Network Software."

Although you have to open the case of a desktop computer to install an internal network adapter card, the job isn't difficult. The basic procedure for installing an internal adapter card is the same on PCs and Macs.

Internal Adapters for Desktop Computers

To install an internal adapter card on a PC or Mac:

1. Shut down the computer.

2. Remove the computer's cover. For a minitower computer, lay the computer down on its side after you remove the cover.

Removing the cover may be easy or difficult, depending on its design. You may have to press latches, twist or pry off fasteners, or remove screws. If you need specific instructions for removing the cover, check the manual that came with your computer.

> If you remove any screws or fasteners, put them in a cup, egg carton, or plastic bag so they don't get lost.

3. Discharge any static electricity your body might be storing by touching the computer's power supply (the big metal box inside the computer). You can also touch the unpainted part of a metal lamp.

4. Unplug the power cord from the computer.

5. Locate an unused expansion slot of the same type as the adapter card. The slots are lined up at the back of the computer. Your adapter card will fit in only one kind of slot, so you can't accidentally put it in the wrong one.

6. Remove the thin metal cover at the back of the expansion slot to allow access to the card from the outside of the computer. You may have to remove a screw. Do what you like with the slot cover, but don't lose the screw!

> Now, before installing the card, check the card's manual to see if you need to set switches or jumpers. These days, most network cards don't require you to do this, but some still do.

7. Insert the card into the slot. Make sure the connector on the bottom edge of the card is lined up with the slot, and firmly press straight down.

8. Use the screw that you saved when you removed the slot cover (step 6) to screw in the card.

9. Replace the computer cover and reconnect the power cord.

Before you can use a newly installed network adapter card, you may need to install driver software for it. In addition, you need to set up the network software on the computer. We cover these procedures in

Chapter 3, "Set Up Your Windows Network Software" and Chapter 4, "Set Up Your Mac Network Software."

Attaching a Transceiver: Macs Only

If you have a Mac with just an AAUI connector and have not yet attached a transceiver, you need to do this. The transceiver has a cable that plugs into the AAUI connector on the back of the Mac. You don't have to install any software to use a transceiver, but you do have to set up the network software as described in Chapter 4, "Set Up Your Mac Network Software."

Connecting the Computers

When each of your networked computers has a connector for 10BaseT or 10/100BaseT, you're ready to hook up the network cables. Unless you're connecting only two computers and have decided to use a crossover cable, you need to connect everything to your hub.

To connect a network with a hub:

The computers don't have to be turned off when you plug in your network cables.

1. Place the hub in a central location. Plug in the hub's power cord, if it has one; or plug the hub into a computer, if it is designed to do so. If the hub has a power switch, turn it on.

2. If you have installed jacks near the hub, run a patch cable from each jack to any unused port on the hub.

3. If you have installed a network jack near a computer or other network device, run a patch cable from its Ethernet connector to the jack.

4. If you have a computer or another network device that is not near a jack, run a network cable from its Ethernet connector to any unused port on the hub.

To connect a network without a hub:

- Connect the two computers by running a crossover cable between their Ethernet connectors.

Installing a LocalTalk Network

Although big ol' LocalTalk networks with all the complexity of a big Ethernet network aren't unheard of, a small LocalTalk network is a whole lot simpler to install. LocalTalk makes a great impromptu network —carry around a phone cord and a couple of small connector boxes with your Mac PowerBook, and you can connect to just about any Mac in a few seconds.

You can also install a more permanent LocalTalk network. In this case, you should spend some time planning the wiring configuration. Wiring considerations for LocalTalk are pretty much the same as for Ethernet, except a LocalTalk network doesn't need a hub. If you haven't already read "Planning the Wiring" earlier in this chapter, take a few minutes to read it now.

With LocalTalk, your network may be able to connect to and use the telephone wires that are already installed inside your walls. Most conventional in-wall telephone cables have two pairs of wires: Your telephone uses one pair, and LocalTalk can probably use the other pair. (Sometimes a second phone line uses the other pair, but more often a second phone line has its own cable.) You won't have to do any wiring to extend your LocalTalk network from room to room; simply plug LocalTalk into a phone jack and it's ready to go.

Check the Phone Wires: To see whether your existing phone wiring has a spare pair of wires that you can use for LocalTalk, grab a screwdriver and remove the cover from a phone jack. If you see four colored wires—red, green, yellow, and black—exiting from the phone cable inside the jack, you're in good shape. Your telephone should be connected to the red and green pair of wires; LocalTalk will use the yellow and black pair.

Each Mac needs an inexpensive LocalTalk connector. The most common brand is Farallon's PhoneNet connectors. In fact, the PhoneNet brand name is so common that all LocalTalk connectors are often referred to as PhoneNet connectors. Note that Apple's original LocalTalk connectors and cables cost more than PhoneNet-style connectors and phone cords.

LocalTalk connectors come in two configurations: The garden-variety setup is a small box with a short cable on one side and two phone jacks on the other side. The short cable plugs into the Mac, and you plug ordinary phone cords into the phone jacks. The phone cords go to LocalTalk connectors of other Macs or printers. The other type of LocalTalk connector is a compact unit with a single phone jack. The compact connector can be used only at the end of a LocalTalk daisy chain.

Hubs of Yore
LocalTalk hubs do exist in large older networks, but any new network with enough computers to justify a hub should use Ethernet. Your small LocalTalk network will not need a hub.

What You Need

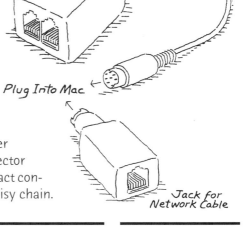

Jacks for Network Cables

Plug Into Mac

Jack for Network Cable

The phone cords you run from one LocalTalk connector to the next must have **four conductors** (those little colored wires that you can see inside the clear plastic plug). This is the most common kind of phone cord and the one packaged with most brands of LocalTalk connectors. If you use a two-conductor cord, your network won't work.

Hooking Up the Pieces

Connecting a LocalTalk network is as easy as plugging in telephones.

To connect a LocalTalk network:

1. Plug a LocalTalk connector into each Mac's Printer port—the port labeled with a printer icon. Some PowerBook models and some desktop Macs with internal modems have a combination Printer/Modem port; plug the LocalTalk connector into that.

   You can connect a LocalTalk printer instead of a Mac anywhere in the chain. Many of Apple's LaserWriter printers are LocalTalk printers.

2. Run a phone cord from each Mac's LocalTalk connector to the next Mac's LocalTalk connector, creating a daisy chain of Macs. When you're done, the first and last Macs in the chain should have only one phone cord plugged into their LocalTalk connectors. If you have only two Macs, the same phone cord plugs into both of their LocalTalk connectors—one end of the cord plugs into one LocalTalk connector, and the other end of the cord plugs into the other connector.

   Make sure you don't make the daisy chain a closed loop by running a phone cord from one end of the chain to the other. The network won't work if you do.

3. Insert a terminating plug into the spare jack of the LocalTalk connector at each end of the daisy chain. This keeps network signals from being reflected back along the cable and hampering network performance.

   A terminating plug should be included with each LocalTalk connector that has two jacks. If you use a single-jack connector at the end of a daisy chain, you don't need a terminating plug.

4. If you're using existing phone wiring for your LocalTalk network, you can run a phone cord from each Mac's LocalTalk connector to a phone jack. Or you can daisy-chain some Macs and connect either the first or the last Mac in the chain to a phone jack. But

don't connect both the first and the last Macs in a chain to phone jacks, or you'll make the daisy chain a closed loop. If there's only one Mac in the room, run a phone cord from its LocalTalk connector to a phone jack.

You don't have to install any software for a LocalTalk network (it's all included with the Mac OS), but you do have to set up the network software as described in Chapter 4.

Maybe you loathe the thought of installing Ethernet wiring and consider LocalTalk quite beyond the pale. You want to believe the media hype that said phone-line, power-line, and wireless networks would take all the work out of installing a network. Although it's true that using them can help you avoid the hassle of installing new wiring, reviewers found that the first batch of products for these alternative networks were too hard to get up and running. Networks based on these products could be unstable, erratic, and just plain unworkable. We hope the second or third round of phone-line, power-line, and wireless network products will be more reliable.

Since we recommend you stick with Ethernet or LocalTalk for your small network, we're not going to cover phone-line, power-line, or wireless network installation in this book. Of course, if you're the kind of person who likes to experiment, you can buy kits that provide the hardware, software, and some of the information you need to hook up these alternative networks. Good luck!

If you successfully install a phone-line, power-line, or wireless network—congratulations! Skip to Part 2 of this book, where you'll read about the many services any small local network can provide no matter what the physical means of connection.

Installing a Phone-Line, Power-Line, or Wireless Network

First Generation Isn't Ready for Prime Time

Summary

In this chapter, you learned about the different kinds of networks you can install, how to plan your network installation, and how to install network equipment. Installing a network takes some effort, but you need to do it only once.

▼ A **10BaseT Ethernet** network is the most common type of network for PCs and Macs. It requires special wiring but has plenty of speed for almost all network services.

▼ A **100BaseT Ethernet** network uses costlier network hardware than 10BaseT, to move more data and move it faster across the network. The extra speed and capacity lets the network handle video, sound, and large graphics.

▼ A **LocalTalk** network is inexpensive and easy to install but is essentially for older Macs only. It's much slower than 10BaseT Ethernet, but LocalTalk is fast enough for sharing printers, some files, and an Internet connection.

▼ **Alternative phone-line, power-line, and wireless networks** are quite a bit slower than Ethernet. You don't have to worry about wires, but reliability problems may actually make them harder to get working.

▼ **Installing a 10BaseT or 100BaseT Ethernet** network involves planning the wiring, buying the network hardware, installing network adapters in computers as needed, and running the wires.

▼ **Installing a LocalTalk** (mostly Macintosh) network requires some planning and wiring as well, but it's less effort than Ethernet installation. You plug a connector into each Mac and run phone cords from one connector to another.

Set Up Your Windows Network Software

After you install the network hardware in a PC, you'll need to install and configure the Windows network software so that your computer can contact other computers on your network. Installing this software is kind of like putting tires on a new bicycle. Without the tires, the bike's mechanism will work, but the bike won't go anywhere. When you install the appropriate Windows software, you're doing the equivalent of putting air in the tires at the right pressure and then adjusting the chain—but you won't get your hands dirty!

Windows Networking Software

When you set up Windows network software, you encounter four network software components:

- The **adapter driver** enables Windows to control the specific model of network adapter card that's installed in the computer.

- **Protocols** are the network languages that computers use to communicate.

- **Client software** enables a PC to connect to other computers and use shared files, printers, and other resources.

- Through a PC's **service software**, other machines can connect to that PC and use its shared files, a shared printer, and other resources.

Plug and Play Software Installation

In this chapter we'll take a look at the settings and options for the adapter driver, protocols, client elements, and services of Windows networking software. Later, in Part Two, we'll explore many kinds of service software in more detail.

The first time you start a computer after installing a network adapter card that's compatible with the Windows **Plug and Play** feature (as described in Chapter 2), Windows 95 or 98 detects the new adapter card and installs the correct driver software for the adapter.

We're assuming the network adapter cards that you installed in Chapter 2 are compatible with the Windows Plug and Play feature. If that's not the case, you'll have to follow the instructions that came with each adapter card to install the cards—good luck!

The sequence of events that occur depends on whether Windows can find the driver software for the model of network adapter card that's installed in the computer.

Found it!

- If Windows 95/98 locates driver software for the new adapter card, you don't have to do a thing. Windows automatically installs the driver software, as shown here in the New Hardware Found window.

Windows automatically installs driver software for a new Plug and Play network adapter.

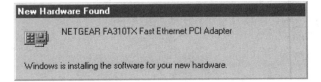

New Hardware Found

NETGEAR FA310TX Fast Ethernet PCI Adapter

Windows is installing the software for your new hardware.

- Windows may determine that it needs to copy driver software from the Windows CD-ROM (or from one of the Windows installation disks). Insert the CD (or disk) when the program requests it and then click OK. Windows installs the driver software from the CD (or disk).

Need the driver, please!

- If Windows can't determine which driver software to use for the new network adapter card, a dialog box opens and lists the options available. Select the appropriate option, and click OK to have Windows install the driver you selected. For advice on the option you need to select, check the instructions that came with the adapter card.

More instructions, please!

Although Windows generally does a pretty good job of installing the network software for a Plug and Play network adapter, you still need to check its work. You may need to install a missing network software component or change some settings. You'll use the Network dialog box to install and set up most of the Windows network.

The Network Dialog Box

To open the Network dialog box:

1. Click the Start button, point to Settings, and then click Control Panel. The Control Panel window opens.

2. Double-click the Network icon to reveal the Network dialog box.

Network

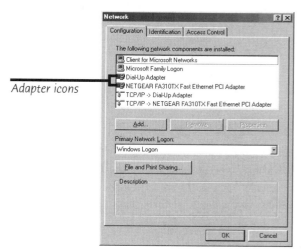

Adapter icons

The Network dialog box lists installed network components (yours are likely to be different from the ones shown here) and lets you set their options.

> ### Protocol and Client Installation
>
> *Along with driver software for the new Plug and Play network adapter, Windows may automatically install protocol and client software, too. You'll read more about this later in this chapter.*

You can open the Network dialog box in several ways. A quick method is to right-click the Network Neighborhood icon on the desktop, and then choose Properties from the shortcut menu that pops up. If you like using icons better than menus, double-click the My Computer icon on the desktop, then double-click the Control Panel icon, and finally double-click the Network icon.

The Configuration Tab

The first tab of the Network dialog box is the **Configuration tab**, which lists the **network components** that are already installed on your system and lets you add or remove others. You can also click the **Properties** button to change the properties of the components. This dialog may contain other tabs, depending on the version of Windows you're using and on which network software is already installed.

In case you're wondering how the installed network components got there, some of them were probably installed when Windows was installed (via the Plug and Play feature). You don't have to re-install network components that are already installed. You *do* need to make sure all the necessary network components are there and are set up properly, as explained in the rest of this chapter.

Keep your Windows CD-ROM (or disks) handy. When you install a missing network software component and close the Network dialog box, you may be prompted to insert the Windows CD-ROM.

Configuring the Network Adapter

The first thing you should do in the Network dialog box is check whether your network adapter is set up correctly. With a Plug and Play network adapter, the correct settings are most likely already in place. However, occasionally Windows doesn't get everything right.

To check your network adapter settings:

1. Open the Network dialog box and make sure the Configuration tab is showing. You should see your network adapter card listed in the installed components list. Adapters are marked in the list with a green icon that looks like a circuit board.

The part of this icon that looks like a capital P actually represents electronic chips and the card's edge connector.

You may see other adapters listed, even if the computer has only one network adapter card installed. For example, if the computer is set up to make an Internet connection via modem, you will see Dial-Up Adapter in the list. Windows considers many things to be "network adapters." For now, focus on the adapter card to which your local network is connected.

2. If your adapter card is listed, skip ahead to the section "Checking the Adapter Settings." Otherwise, march on, and add your adapter to the configuration.

Network Adapter

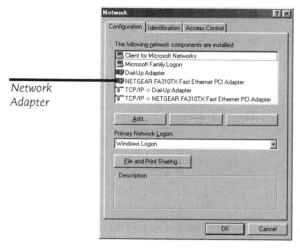

Make sure the network adapter card is listed.

If you don't see your network adapter in the list of installed network components in the Network dialog box, you'll have to add your adapter. Windows calls this "adding a network adapter," but what you're really doing is adding the *driver software* for the adapter.

To add a network adapter (driver software):

1. In the Network dialog box Configuration tab, click the Add button. The Select Network Component Type dialog box appears, as shown here.

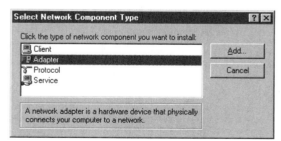

You can add an adapter to your configuration in this dialog box.

Adding a Network Adapter

Remember: You can open the Network dialog box from the Control Panel, or through the Network Neighborhood or My Computer icon on the desktop.

2. Click Adapter in the list of network components, and then click the Add button to open the Select Network Adapters dialog box.

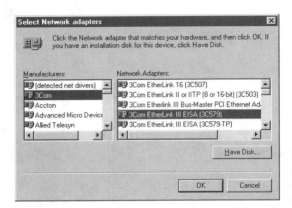

Select your network adapter's make and model, or click the Have Disk button.

3. Do one of the following:

▼ **If you don't have an installation disk for your network adapter** or you don't want to use the disk, look in the list on the left for the name of your network adapter's manufacturer and click the manufacturer's name. In the list on the right, click the name of the adapter model. Click OK when you're done, and continue to step 4.

▼ **If you have the installation disk that came with your network adapter,** click the Have Disk button. The Install From Disk dialog box appears next, prompting you to insert the installation disk. Make sure the correct drive is designated in the dialog box. (For instance, if you're inserting a floppy disk, make sure **A:** is designated.)

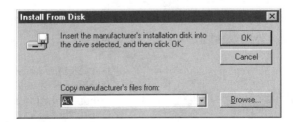

Make sure the correct disk drive is designated.

4. Click OK, and you'll see a listing of the network adapters for which driver software exists on the installation disk, as shown in the next figure. Click the name of your adapter in this list and then click OK.

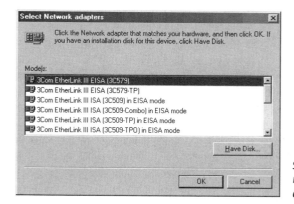

Select your
network adapter
and click OK.

5. The network adapter you selected is now listed at the top of the Configuration tab. However, the adapter is not set up yet. You can set up now or wait until later:

▼ If you want to continue setting up the network software now, continue to the next section, "Checking the Adapter Settings."

▼ If you want to take a break from setting up the network software, click OK in the Network dialog box. You may be prompted to insert the disk that came with network adapter, or the Windows CD-ROM so that files can be copied from it. When file copying is complete, the Network dialog box closes and the System Settings Change dialog box advises you to restart your computer. Click Yes to restart.

Clicking the Close (X) button in the upper-right corner of the Network dialog box has the same effect as clicking the Cancel button. If you click either of these buttons, the dialog box closes and none of your changes will take effect.

Checking the Adapter Settings

Once your network adapter is listed at the top of the Configurations tab's list of installed components, you can check the adapter's settings to make sure they are all correct. You can do this in the **Adapter Properties** dialog box.

1. If you're resuming after a break and the Network dialog box is closed, open it again.

2. In the Configuration tab, scroll through the list of network components until you see the name of your network adapter. Click it to select it.

3. Click the Properties button. This opens the selected adapter's Properties dialog box, which contains several tabs.

   Here's a Windows shortcut: Double-click an item in the Network dialog box components list to open the Properties dialog box.

Designating the ***Driver Type***

4. On the Driver Type tab of the Properties dialog box, make sure that the Enhanced Mode (32-bit and 16-bit) NDIS Driver option is selected.

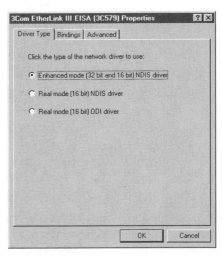

Select the Enhanced Mode driver for the adapter.

Binding *a protocol to a network adapter enables the adapter to use that protocol.*

5. Click the Bindings tab to open it.

6. In the Bindings tab, select the network protocols you want the adapter to use. If you're not sure now which protocols to select, go ahead and select all that are available. (We'll talk more about protocols later in this chapter.)

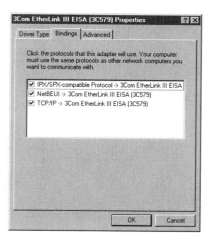

Select the protocols you want the adapter to use.

7. You're now finished setting up the network adapter. At this point, you may want to take a break.

   ▼ If you want to stop here, click OK in the Network dialog box. You may be prompted to insert your Windows CD-ROM so files can be copied from it.

   ▼ If you want to push on, keep the Network dialog box open.

In addition to setting up the network adapter, you need to make sure the Microsoft **client software** is installed. The client software shows you which of the other network computers have shared printers and files. When you want to connect to one of these computers, the client software displays a dialog box in which you identify yourself and enter your password. Then your PC uses the client software to contact the other computer and ask its permission for you to connect.

The Microsoft client software may have been installed automatically when Windows first detected the computer's Plug and Play network adapter. If not, you can install the client software using the Network dialog box and your Windows CD-ROM (or Windows disks).

To see whether the client software is installed:

1. If necessary, open the Network dialog box.

2. In the Configuration tab's list of installed components, look for Client for Microsoft Networks. If it's there, the client software is already installed on your PC. You can skip to the section, "Checking the Client Settings." If the client software is missing, you should add it now.

Installing the Client Software

To install the client software:

1. Click the Add button on the Configurations tab of the Network dialog box. This opens the Select Network Component Type dialog box, shown below.

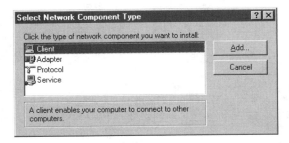

Choose the type of network component you want to install in this dialog box.

2. Click Client and then click the Add button to open the Select Network Client dialog box.

3. In the list of manufacturers on the left, click Microsoft. In the list of clients on the right, click Client for Microsoft Networks. As the name suggests, this is the standard client software for Windows networks. You don't need to bother with other client software listed here.

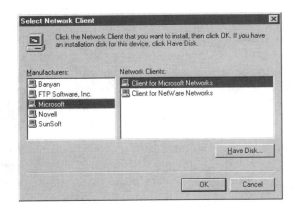

Click to select the client software for Microsoft networks.

4. Click OK. You now see Client for Microsoft Networks in the list at the top of the Configuration tab.

When you see that the Microsoft client has been installed, you can set the properties in the **Client Properties** dialog box. These include Logon Validation and Network Logon Options.

Checking the Client Settings

1. In the Configurations tab of the Network dialog box, click Client for Microsoft Networks in the list of components. Then click the Properties button. (Or simply double-click Client for Microsoft Networks.) The Properties dialog box for the Microsoft client software appears.

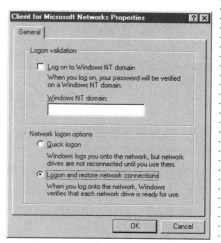

Set the client software properties in this dialog box.

2. Click to select one of the radio button options in the Network Logon Options section of the Properties dialog box. These options determine when Windows will connect to other computers and network printers.

Network Logon Options

   ▼ **If you click Quick Logon,** Windows will connect to network computers and printers as you use them. This is usually the best option for small networks.

   ▼ **If you click Logon and Restore Network Connections,** Windows will try to restore all network connections every time it starts up. This increases Windows' startup time, but it might be useful if your network consists largely of laptop computers that are not always connected to the network.

   If you're not sure whether to select Quick Logon or Logon and Restore, pick one and try it out for a while. If it doesn't work correctly, you can open the Network dialog box and change the setting at any time.

You can ignore the Logon Validation section of the Properties dialog box unless your network has a Windows NT server (a scenario not covered in this book).

Logon Validation

3. If you do have a Windows NT server on the network, click the Log On to Windows NT Domain check box to activate it. If you've set up Windows NT domains on the server, type the name of the domain to which your PC belongs into the text box provided.

4. Click OK to close the Properties dialog box and apply your settings.

Take a breather, or press on.

This concludes the setup of the Microsoft client software. You will, however, return to the Network dialog box in later chapters to install and set up additional client software. At this point, you have two options:

▼ If you want continue setting up the Windows network software, proceed to the next section, "Choosing Protocols."

▼ If you've had enough of the Network dialog box for a while, click its OK button to close it and take a breather. A message box may ask you to insert the Windows CD-ROM so that Windows can copy files from it to your hard disk.

Choosing Protocols

The Microsoft client software installed on your network is "multi-lingual." That is, it can use more than one **protocol**, which is a set of rules that computers use to communicate on a network.

For two computers to communicate on a network, they must use the same protocol. The client software on one computer knows which protocols it can use to contact service software on another computer. For example, Client for Microsoft Networks (which you have just finished setting up) knows which protocols it can use to contact the service software for file and printer sharing on another computer.

Each computer may have multiple clients, and all these clients may use various, multiple protocols. For example, Client for Microsoft Networks may use one protocol for printer sharing and file sharing, while another client on the same computer uses another protocol for everything on the Internet.

Speaking of Protocols...

Think of protocols as languages. When you talk to someone, you both speak the same language, but that doesn't prevent you from speaking with other people in other languages.

Windows 95 and 98 supply a whole slew of protocols. The most popular protocols among Windows computers are NetBEUI, TCP/IP, and IPX/SPX. Earlier in the chapter, you verified your network adapter's bindings to make sure your computer is set up to use one or more of these three network protocols. So which ones does your computer really need? The answer depends on what you want to do with your network and on how easy or hard it is to set up the protocols.

SERVICES/ACTIVITIES   *WINDOWS 95/98*
                               PROTOCOLS/LANGUAGES

TCP/IP OR IPX/SPX

TCP/IP ONLY

TCP/IP OR NETBEUI

TCP/IP OR NETBEUI

NetBEUI is fast and easy. It's one of the protocols that Client for Microsoft Networks can use for sharing printers and files on a small Windows network. Other client software can use it as well. NetBEUI is easy to set up. In fact, you can leave the default settings as they are.

NetBEUI

NetBEUI's disadvantage is that you can't use it to share files and printers with Macintosh computers on your network. If that's something you want to do, ignore NetBEUI and make sure TCP/IP is installed. Another draw-back of NetBEUI probably won't concern you much: Its use is limited to small networks—for practical purposes, that's 20 to 30 computers.

The versatile **TCP/IP** is the protocol for all Internet services; it can also be used for local network services. Client for Microsoft Networks can use TCP/IP for sharing printers and files, and TCP/IP is the *only* way you can share files and printers among Windows and Macintosh computers. In addition, some games use TCP/IP for multiplayer action. And you'll definitely use TCP/IP if you want to share an Internet account.

TCP/IP

On the downside, TCP/IP is harder to set up than NetBEUI. If you're going to share printers and files among Windows computers only, you might just skip TCP/IP and use NetBEUI as your network protocol.

IPX/SPX   **IPX/SPX** is the protocol used by some games—instead of TCP/IP—to enable multiplayer action via the network. This protocol is also used by older versions of Novell NetWare, a type of network that requires dedicated servers. (Current versions of NetWare use TCP/IP.)

Checking Installed Protocols   At this point in setting up your Windows network software, one or more protocols will already be installed on your computer. "Where did they come from?" you might ask. You already know that some protocols are normally installed when Windows itself is installed. TCP/IP is installed as part of Windows 98, and IPX/SPX and NetBEUI come with Windows 95. As mentioned earlier, protocols are also installed quite often when the Plug and Play feature installs the adapter driver.

You can find out which protocols are installed on your computer by looking in the same Network dialog box that you've already used several times in this chapter. Look in the Configuration tab; installed protocols are included in the list of installed components.

Take a look at the Network dialog box shown below. Protocols are marked in the list with an icon that resembles network cables (use your imagination), but the dead giveaway is the name of the protocol in the list. Each protocol name is followed by the name of a network adapter, and an arrowlike symbol between the two names means this protocol is bound to this adapter. You may see a protocol listed more than once, each time with a different adapter. Each listing represents a different binding. (Recall that Windows considers many things besides network interface cards to be adapters.)

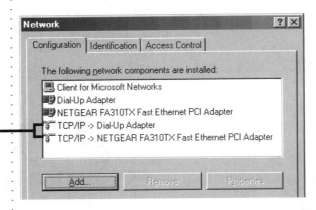

Protocols

Check to see whether the protocols you need are installed.

If the protocol you need isn't listed in the Configuration tab of the Network dialog box, you can add it.

To add a protocol:

1. If necessary, open the Configuration tab of the Network dialog box.

2. Click the Add button to open the Select Network Component Type dialog box (which you've seen earlier in this chapter).

3. Select Protocol, and then click the Add button. The Select Network Protocol dialog box appears.

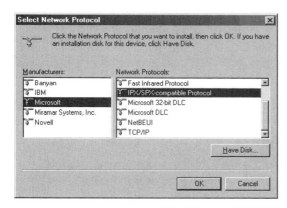

Select Microsoft from the list on the left, and then select the protocol you want to add from the list on the right.

4. Select Microsoft from the Manufacturers list on the left, and select the protocol you want to add from the list on the right.

5. Click OK.

   You'll see the chosen protocol listed (along with the name of your adapter) in the components list of the Configuration tab.

6. If you want to add another protocol, repeat steps 2 through 5.

   The protocols you've added are not fully installed until you click OK to close the Network dialog box. But you don't have to do that yet.

   ▼ To keep going, continue to the next section, "Configuring NetBEUI or IPX/SPX."

   ▼ To stop for a while, click OK at the bottom of the Network dialog box. Windows will begin copying files, and may ask you to insert the Windows installation CD-ROM so that files can be copied from it. At the end of this process, a System Settings Change dialog box asks if you want to restart the computer. Click Yes.

Configuring NetBEUI or IPX/SPX

The protocols that you have added, as well as the protocols that you found already installed, all have settings that can be changed. NetBEUI and IPX/SPX, however, have only a few settings, and they're configured properly when these protocols are installed.

If you're not sure whether NetBEUI or IPX/SPX are configured properly—perhaps you bought the computer secondhand and you suspect someone may have messed with the protocol settings in the past—the simplest cure is to remove the protocol in question from the Network dialog box and then add it back in. Re-installing NetBEUI or IPX/SPX in this manner resets the protocol to work properly in a small network.

To remove a protocol:

1. Look in the list of installed components at the top of the Network dialog box's Configuration tab.

2. Select the listing for the protocol you want to remove. (If you see more than one listing for the same protocol, select any one of them.)

3. Click the Remove button.

4. Repeat steps 2 and 3 if the protocol you are removing has other listings remaining in the Network dialog box.

Reinstalling Protocols

After removing all instances of NetBEUI or IPX/SPX from the Network dialog box, install the protocol again as described in the preceding section, "Adding Protocols."

Protocol Overpopulation: Don't add NetBEUI or IPX/SPX without first removing all instances of the protocol, or you may simply end up with more instances of the same protocol. If this happens, remove *all* instances of the protocol from the Configuration tab of the Network dialog box, and then add the protocol back in as directed earlier.

Configuring TCP/IP for a Local Network

In contrast to NetBEUI and IPX/SPX, TCP/IP may give you a bit of trouble during setup. You may need to change some standard TCP/IP settings so this protocol will work on your small local network. Your configuration tasks will center on making sure each computer on the network has its own address.

A computer may already have a separate TCP/IP configuration for the Internet, but this configuration is independent of the TCP/IP configuration for your local network. For now, you can focus on the TCP/IP configuration for the network adapter to which your local network connects.

Every computer that uses TCP/IP must have a unique **IP address**. On some networks, every computer is assigned an IP address automatically, but on small networks it's often necessary to assign IP addresses manually. You will need to manually assign an IP address to each computer on your network that uses Windows 95. You can also assign IP addresses manually for computers that use Windows 98, or you can let these computers assign their own IP addresses.

It's also possible to have a special program running on one computer on the network to automatically assign each computer an IP address as the computer joins the network. (Normally, a computer joins the network automatically every time it starts up.) This program is called a **DHCP server** (short for dynamic host configuration protocol). Chapter 5 describes one way you can add a DHCP server to your network.

Whether manually or automatically assigned, each IP address consists of four numbers with a period between each number. Each number in the address must be between 0 and 255. Here's an example of a typical IP address: 169.254.254.1

Use IP Addresses Reserved for Local Networks:
Although you can use any IP addresses you like on your local network, it's best to use addresses that are approved and set aside for private TCP/IP networks. That way, if you provide Internet access on your local network, your local IP addresses won't get mixed up with the IP addresses of computers on the Internet. The private IP addresses will be used only on your local network, and the IP address assigned by your Internet service provider will be used on the Internet. (We'll cover IP addresses and the Internet in Chapter 5.)

Several ranges of IP address numbers have been designated for local networks. For best compatibility with Windows 98, as well as with any Macintosh computers using Mac OS 8.5 or later on your network, you should use addresses that look like this: 169.254.x.y, where x and y are numbers between 0 and 255. Each computer must have a different value for x or y. For example, you could assign your computers the addresses 169.254.101.1, 169.254.101.2, 169.254.101.3, and so on. In this range of IP addresses, the numbers 169.254 identify your local network, and the last two numbers of each address uniquely identify one computer or other device that uses the network.

About IP Addresses

Rules of IP Addressing

IP Address Numbers

Internet Addresses
You don't normally see IP addresses on the Internet because an Internet service converts alphabetic addresses, such as www.peachpit.com, to numeric IP addresses.

Self-Assigned IP Address

You need to specify how the PC will get its unique IP address. If the PC uses Windows 98, it can assign itself an IP address. In fact, when you install the network software, it will be set up to do just that. Every time the PC starts up or restarts, Windows 98 assigns it an IP number from the range 169.254.0.0 through 169.254.254.255. However, Windows 98 does not assign an IP address if your network has a DHCP server; in that case, the DHCP server assigns an IP address (more in Chapter 5).

To confirm that Windows 98 is configured to self-assign an IP address:

1. In the Configuration tab of the Network dialog box, look in the list of installed components. Select the listing that combines TCP/IP and the adapter to which your local network connects.

2. Click the Properties button. The TCP/IP Properties box will open with the IP Address tab on top.

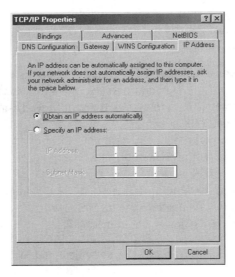

Confirming that Windows 98 will self-assign an IP address.

3. Make sure the option Obtain an IP Address Automatically is selected. (This is the same setting you would choose if your network had a DHCP server.)

4. Click OK to close the TCP/IP Properties window.

5. To finish setting up the Windows network software, proceed now to the section "Naming the Computer."

▼ To take a break, click OK in the Network dialog box. You may be asked to insert your Windows CD-ROM so files can be copied from it, and you may be asked to restart the computer.

If you have Windows 95 machines on the network, you'll have to manu- ally assign their IP addresses. You can enter an IP address manually for any Windows 98 machine as well, if you want to. Fortunately, you can mix manual and self-assigned addressing on the computers in your network.

Entering an IP Address Manually

To enter an IP address manually:

1. In the Network dialog box, select the Configuration tab.

2. In the list of installed components, select the listing that combines TCP/IP with the adapter used by your local network, and then click the Properties button. The TCP/IP Properties dialog box for your network card opens, with the IP Address tab forward.

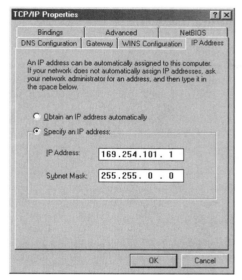

Manually entering an IP address and subnet mask number.

3. Select the option Specify an IP Address.

4. In the text box labeled IP Address, enter an IP address that begins with **169.254** and ends with two numbers, each between 0 and 255, that you have not assigned to any other computer on your network. The first two numbers of this IP address identify your local net- work, and the last two numbers of the IP address identify a particular machine on the network.

5. In the Subnet Mask text box, enter **255.255.0.0**

The subnet mask gets its name from the fact that it can also be used to divide a TCP/IP network into subnetworks. The value 255.255.0.0 indicates that your small TCP/IP network has no subnetworks.

6. Click the OK button to close the TCP/IP Properties window.

▼ If you want to stop working in the Network dialog box, click OK; be prepared to insert the Windows CD-ROM and restart the computer. Otherwise, continue to the next section.

Naming the Computer

Name the computer so it can be recognized by other people on the network.

1. In the Network dialog box, click the Identification tab.

2. Type a computer name in the top field. You can name the computer anything you want, but it's helpful for the other people on the network if you use something that will easily identify the machine, such as "Bob's PC" or "Art room computer."

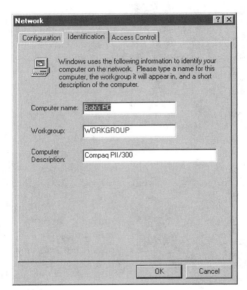

Give the computer a name in the Identification tab.

3. Leave the word WORKGROUP in the second field.

If you'd rather change the Workgroup name to something more interesting, go ahead. Just be sure you use the same workgroup name for all of your PCs.

4. In the last field, you can describe the computer. This can be a model name or number, a description of the computer's location, or something as simple as "Bob's computer."

5. Click the OK button to close the Network dialog box. Windows may ask you to insert the Windows CD, and then it will ask you if you want to restart the PC. Click Yes.

Summary

After connecting a PC to your local network, you need to configure the PC network software. In this chapter, we've explained how to do that. Let's review the main points:

▼ Windows 95 and 98 have four network software components: **adapter drivers, protocols, clients, and services**.

▼ After you install a **Plug and Play** network adapter, Windows 95 or 98 detects it and automatically installs the necessary network software components.

▼ You configure your network software from the **Network dialog box**.

▼ In the network adapter's **Properties** dialog box, check the adapter's driver type and its binding to network protocols.

▼ You need to install the **client software** to share printers and files.

▼ PCs can use multiple network protocols, including **NetBEUI, TCP/IP, and IPX/SPX**. You can use NetBEUI and IPX/SPX without changing any of the default settings.

▼ On a small local TCP/IP network, each computer should have a different **IP address** in the range 169.254.0.0 to 169.254.255.255.

▼ This **IP address** is only for the network adapter to which your local network connects. This address will not be used or affected by a dial-up connection to the Internet.

▼ **Windows 98 can self-assign** an IP address, or you can manually enter one. You must **manually enter an IP address in Windows 95**.

▼ If you manually enter an IP address that begins 169.254, you must also enter a **subnet mask** of 255.255.0.0.

▼ Name a computer in the **Identification** tab of the Network dialog box.

Set Up Your Mac Network Software 4

After you connect a Mac to your local network, you need to make sure the Mac's network software is configured correctly. If it's not, your Mac will be unable to contact other computers and devices on the local network. This is comparable to configuring the switches and dials on a stereo system after hooking up the receiver, speakers, CD player, and other components. To hear a CD, you've got to turn on the system and set the selector switch to route the CD player signal through the receiver to the speakers. On a Mac, you do the equivalent of setting these switches and dials by setting options in the Chooser and in a couple of control panels.

Mac OS Network Software

It's likely that you won't have to install any Mac network software at all. Most of the software you need for a Mac connected to a small network is handily included in the Mac OS.

Apple Built-In Ethernet

For instance, the Mac OS includes the driver software you need for a **built-in Ethernet port**. If your network connects to a Mac's built-in Ethernet port, you don't have to install driver software, and you can skip to the section "Open Transport Software."

You'll also have no driver software to install if you're using a **LocalTalk network**. All the software you need for LocalTalk is included with the Mac OS. If this is the case, you can proceed to the section on Open Transport software.

Add-in Ethernet Adapters

An add-in Ethernet card may require software installation.

If you installed an **Ethernet adapter card** in a desktop Mac or inserted an **Ethernet PC card** into a PowerBook (as described in Chapter 2), and a disk was packaged with the card, that disk probably contains driver software that you should install. Some driver software is installed simply by running an installer program, or you might have to install it yourself by dragging the driver's icon from the disk to the System Folder icon.

For specific installation directions, see the instructions that came with the Ethernet card. If the Ethernet card did not include a disk, you can assume that you don't need to install driver software for it.

Updated Ethernet Drivers

Farallon FastENPlus

If your Ethernet card included its own driver software, you might be able to obtain the most recent version of the driver software from the card's manufacturer. The newer software may improve the card's performance or compatibility with recent Mac OS versions. For example, after Apple released OS 8.5, Farallon released driver software that improves the performance of Farallon's Ethernet cards when they are used with Mac OS 8.5 and later.

To check on the availability of updated driver software, call the technical support department of the Ethernet card's manufacturer, or check the manufacturer's Web site.

Open Transport Software

Recent versions of the Mac OS incorporate the second generation of Mac network software, called **Open Transport**. Open Transport software is faster and more reliable than its predecessor, now known as **Classic Networking**. Most Macs already have Open Transport networking software or can be upgraded to use it, and that's the networking system we describe in this chapter.

Setting up the Mac network software is quite different from setting up a Windows PC in a Windows network (Chapter 3). If you're using both kinds of machines in your network and if you've read Chapter 3, you'll notice that, except for terms such as *Ethernet* and *TCP/IP,* you won't find much in common between the terminology used in the two chapters. None of the Mac configuration panels look anything like the dialog boxes in Windows.

Not sure whether you're using Open Transport or Classic Networking software? You can find out by opening your Control Panels folder (from the Apple menu, choose Control Panels). If this folder contains the AppleTalk and TCP/IP control panels (shown in the first figure below), you're using Open Transport. If the folder contains Network and MacTCP control panels (shown in the second figure), you're using Classic Networking.

Open Transport vs. Classic Networking

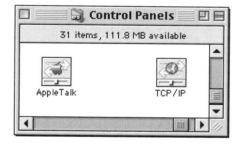

Open Transport control panels.

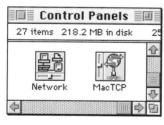

Classic Networking control panels.

If you're currently using Classic Networking on a Mac with **System 7.5.3 or 7.5.5,** you can switch to Open Transport by using the Network Software Selector program located in the Apple Extras folder on your startup disk. Both generations of network software are installed on Macs without PCI expansion slots as part of System 7.5.3 or 7.5.5, and the Network Software Selector activates one while hiding the other.

Updating to Open Transport

If you're using a Mac with **System 7.1, 7.1.1, or 7.1.2**—even though we advised you in Chapter 1 to upgrade to System 7.5.5—you may be able to upgrade to Open Transport separately, without upgrading to a more recent version.

System Requirements for Open Transport

Open Transport works on a Mac with any PowerPC processor and at least 8MB of total memory. Open Transport also works on any Mac with a 68040 or 68030 processor and at least 5MB of total memory. (Total memory includes additional memory provided by the Virtual Memory option in your Memory control panel.) The only Mac models that cannot use Open Transport are Macs with a 68020 or 68000 processor. Open Transport does not work with System 7.5, 7.5.1, or 7.5.2 or System 7.0.1 or earlier. On the other hand, Mac OS 7.6 and later can use only Open Transport (not Classic Networking).

You can get a recent version of Open Transport free from Apple's Software Updates Library on the Internet (*http://www.info.apple.com/swupdates/*). To determine which version of Open Transport you have, open the AppleTalk control panel or the TCP/IP control panel and press Command-I (see the figure below).

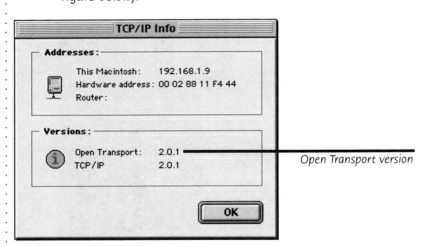

Open Transport version

Whether they use Open Transport or Classic Networking, Macs can communicate with other computers using multiple network languages, or **protocols**. Open Transport is fluent with all network protocols, like a person who grew up bilingual. Classic Networking, on the other hand, like a person who learns a foreign language as an adult, uses **AppleTalk** as its primary protocol, and other protocols (such as **TCP/IP**) are secondary.

Recent versions of the Mac OS (System 7.5 through System 7.5.5, and Mac OS 7.6 and later) include network software for two networking protocols, AppleTalk and TCP/IP. You can use one of the protocols or use both at the same time.

Mac Network Protocols

Use AppleTalk and TCP/IP simultaneously.

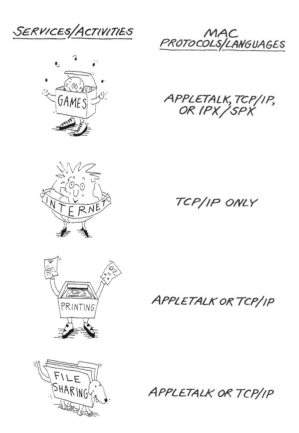

SERVICES/ACTIVITIES

MAC PROTOCOLS/LANGUAGES

GAMES — APPLETALK, TCP/IP, OR IPX/SPX

INTERNET — TCP/IP ONLY

PRINTING — APPLETALK OR TCP/IP

FILE SHARING — APPLETALK OR TCP/IP

AppleTalk　The easy-to-use AppleTalk protocol is the original Macintosh network language. You normally use AppleTalk for sharing files, printers, and other network services among Macs because it is easier to set up and use than TCP/IP. Although AppleTalk is slower than TCP/IP, you won't notice any difference with printing–but you *will* notice it, for example, when you copy a 10MB chunk of files via the network.

We tell you how to set up AppleTalk in the next section, "Setting Up AppleTalk."

TCP/IP　The Mac OS includes software for the TCP/IP protocol because it's the protocol of the Internet. You'll definitely use TCP/IP if you want to share an Internet account. In addition, TCP/IP is a standard protocol for mixed networks that include Macs, Windows PCs, and other computers. Even some Macintosh networking services can now use TCP/IP instead of AppleTalk for improved speed.

Although it's versatile and fast, TCP/IP requires more effort to configure and use than AppleTalk, and you must be careful to get every setting correct. You'll learn why you might want to set up your Mac for TCP/IP on a network, and how to do that setup, in the section "Configuring TCP/IP" a little later in this chapter.

If your network includes more Macs than PCs, you can add AppleTalk to the PCs by installing software such as PC MacLAN from Miramar Systems. (Windows 95 and 98 do not inherently support the AppleTalk protocol.) Adding AppleTalk to Windows is covered in Chapters 6 and 7.

Setting Up AppleTalk　Macs generally use AppleTalk to communicate with network printers such as Apple LaserWriters, to communicate with each other when sharing files, and for most other network communications that involve only Macs. If your network includes Macs, you need to take a few minutes to configure the AppleTalk software on each computer. It's really easy to do: Just make sure the AppleTalk software is active and set to communicate via the port the network cable plugs into. Then you need to make sure each Mac has a name. (You'll learn how to do this later in the chapter in the section "Naming Your Mac.")

Activating AppleTalk　You can check to determine whether AppleTalk is active, and activate it if necessary, using the **Chooser**. This method works on any Mac. Or you can use the Control Strip, if the Mac has one. The following procedures show you how to activate both ways.

To activate AppleTalk from the Chooser:

1. Open the Chooser (click the Apple menu and select Chooser).
To see whether AppleTalk is already active, look in the lower-right
corner of the Chooser window.

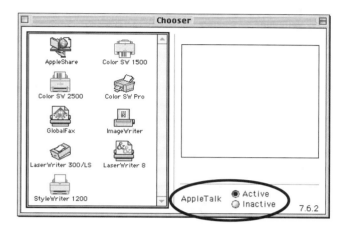

2. If AppleTalk is inactive, click the Active option. An alert box advises
you to make sure your Mac is actually hooked up to a network (you
did this in Chapter 2). Click the OK button to close the alert box.

3. Close the Chooser by clicking its close box or by choosing Close
from the File menu.

You don't have to restart the Mac after making AppleTalk active or
inactive. (If you're using System 7.1 or earlier, however, a message will
appear in the Chooser telling you that AppleTalk will be active on
restart. As discussed earlier in this book, you should upgrade to a more
recent version of the system software.)

Although you can always use the Chooser to activate AppleTalk, on
some Macs there's a quicker way: the **Control Strip**. The Control Strip
is a retractable strip of buttons that help you quickly inspect and
change the settings of many common Mac options, including AppleTalk
activation.

To activate AppleTalk from the Control Strip:

1. Zip open the Control Strip (click or drag its tab so the Control
Strip extends across the screen), and look for the AppleTalk
Switch button. It's normally the leftmost button on the strip, and
its icon looks like a Mac from the mid-1980s. You may have to

scroll to see the AppleTalk Switch button; click the arrow at either end of the Control Strip to do this.

2. Look at the AppleTalk Switch button to determine whether AppleTalk is active. If the button art includes network wires coming out of the bottom of the little computer icon at the bottom, AppleTalk is active:

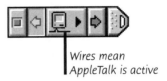

Wires mean
AppleTalk is active

If the button art does not show these network wires, AppleTalk is inactive:

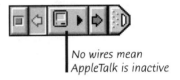

No wires mean
AppleTalk is inactive

3. If AppleTalk is inactive (or if you're not sure), click the AppleTalk Switch button on the Control Strip and choose AppleTalk Active from the pop-up menu.

An alert box advises you to make sure your Mac is actually hooked up to a network (you took care of this in Chapter 2). Click the OK button in the alert box to close it. (This alert does not appear if AppleTalk was already active when you chose AppleTalk Active from the pop-up menu.)

4. Zip the Control Strip closed by clicking on either end, so it retracts to the edge of the screen. (You can leave the Control Strip open if you don't mind giving up the screen space.)

A Mac can use the AppleTalk protocol via one of several ports, so you must specify the port into which the network cable is connected. Follow these steps:

1. From the Apple menu, choose Control Panels.

2. In the Control Panels window, double-click the AppleTalk icon to reveal the AppleTalk control panel, shown below.

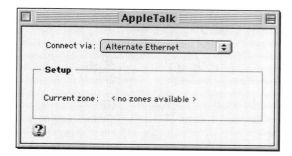

3. Click the Connect Via pop-up menu, and choose the port to which the network is connected (as described in Chapter 2).

   Note that this menu identifies ports by name, but the ports themselves on the Mac are labeled with icons. To help you recognize which port to choose, use the following table. It lists the most common network ports for the AppleTalk protocol.

Port Name on the Connect Via Menu	Type of Connection	Port Icon on the Mac
Ethernet	Built-in Ethernet	⟨⟨∘∘⟩⟩
Alternate Ethernet	Ethernet PC card in a PowerBook	⟨⟨∘∘⟩⟩
Ethernet Slot X	Ethernet adapter card in slot x	⟨⟨∘∘⟩⟩
Printer Port	LocalTalk connector plugged into a port labeled with a printer icon	🖨
Modem Port	LocalTalk connector plugged into a port labeled with a telephone icon	☎
Printer/Modem Port	LocalTalk connector plugged into a port labeled with printer and telephone icons	🖨 ☎
Infrared Port (IrDA) or Infrared Port (IR Talk)	The infrared port that's available on some Mac models	None
Remote Only	A modem connection to a remote network when you want to exclude a simultaneous connection to a local network	None

4. Close the AppleTalk control panel (click its Close box, or choose Close from the File menu).

5. When an alert box asks if you want to save the changes you just made, click the Save button. (This alert does not appear if you did not make any changes before closing the control panel.)

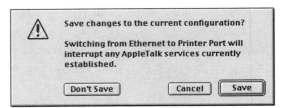

If you see an Info button and an Options button at the bottom of the AppleTalk control panel, it means someone has changed the control panel's user mode from Basic to Advanced or Administration. You can ignore these buttons. Or, if you want to change the user mode, choose User Mode from the Edit menu, select a user mode, and then click OK.

Naming Your Mac

Each Mac using the AppleTalk protocol on a network has a name that identifies it on the network. A Mac's name is especially useful when you're sharing some of its files with other Macs on the network. (We'll get to the subject of file sharing in Chapter 7.) Let's give your Mac a name.

For Networks Using the AppleTalk Protocol

1. Open the appropriate control panel:

If you're using Mac OS 8 or later, open the File Sharing control panel (choose Control Panels from the Apple menu and double-click the File Sharing icon). Click the Start/Stop tab at the top of the control panel.

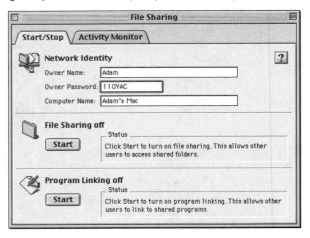

If you're using Mac OS 7.6.1 or earlier, open the Sharing Setup control panel (choose Control Panels from the Apple menu and double-click the Sharing Setup icon).

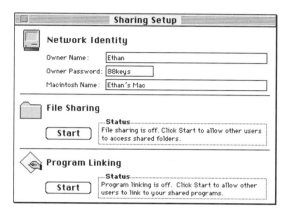

2. Type an Owner Name in the field provided. This is usually the name of the Mac's primary user. You can enter **Napoleon**, **457**, or **Mr. Ed**, if you want to–but a real person's name is usually easier to recognize.

3. Type a password in the Owner Password field. This password is needed only for file sharing.

4. Type a name for this Mac in the Computer Name (or Macintosh Name) field. Again, you can call the Mac anything you want, but a name like **Rita's Macintosh** makes it easy for other people on the network to identify this machine.

> **Changing a Name or Password**: Someone may have already entered a computer name, owner name, and/or password. If you're happy with the current names, you can leave them as is. But if you change either of the names or the password on a particular Mac, be sure to tell the primary user (and the rest of the network users) that you've done so.

In addition to the AppleTalk protocol, the Macs on your local network can use **TCP/IP**, which is the network protocol of the Internet. What's more, some Macintosh network services can now use TCP/IP *instead of* AppleTalk for better performance. For example, you can print to some printers using TCP/IP, access a remote network using TCP/IP, and back up computer files over the network–all faster with TCP/IP than with AppleTalk. You can also use the TCP/IP protocol to share files with

Setting Up TCP/IP

Windows PCs, play games, maintain a group calendar, access a central database, and control a Windows PC.

Eventually, TCP/IP will become more important to Macs than AppleTalk. But for now, if all you're going to do with your network is share printers and files among Macs, you don't need to configure its TCP/IP software for a local network and you can skip the rest of this chapter. If you want to use the Internet or perform more complex functions with your network, forge on.

The following sections explain how to create a TCP/IP configuration specifically for a local network. Since you may also have a separate TCP/IP configuration for the Internet, we'll show you how to switch between the Internet configuration and the local network configuration.

IP Addresses

TCP/IP's versatility and excellent performance contrast with its less appealing side: TCP/IP is more complicated to configure than AppleTalk. With AppleTalk, you always identify computers by name. But with TCP/IP on a small local network, you generally identify computers by number.

Internet Addresses

You don't normally use a numeric IP addresses on the Internet because an Internet service automatically converts the alphabetic address (www.peachpit.com) to a numeric IP address.

The number that identifies a computer in the TCP/IP protocol is called its **IP address**. On some networks, every computer is assigned a unique IP address automatically, but on small networks, it's often necessary for you to assign IP addresses manually.

- **Mac OS 8.1 or earlier**: You'll need to manually assign an IP address to each Mac on your network.
- **Mac OS 8.5 and later**: You can assign IP addresses manually or you can let these Macs assign themselves IP addresses. (Self-assigned IP addresses are a feature of Open Transport 2.0, which was first included with Mac OS 8.5.)

An alternative is to have a special program running on one computer on the network, called a **DHCP server** (short for Dynamic Host Configuration Protocol). The DHCP server automatically assigns an IP address to each computer as it joins the network. (Normally, a computer joins the network automatically every time it starts up.) Chapter 5 describes how you can add a DHCP server to your network.

The Rules of IP Addressing

Whether manually or automatically assigned, each IP address consists of four numbers with a period between each number. Each number in an IP address must be between 0 and 255. Here's an example of an IP address: **169.254.1.254**

Use IP Addresses Reserved for Local Networks:
Although you can use any IP addresses you like on your local
network, it's best to use addresses that are approved and set
aside for private networks using TCP/IP. That way, if you later
provide Internet access on your local network, your local IP
addresses won't get mixed up with the IP addresses of computers on the Internet. The private IP addresses will be used
only on your local network, and the IP address you get from
your Internet service provider will be used on the Internet.
(For more on IP addresses and the Internet, see Chapter 5.)

Several ranges of IP address numbers have been designated for local
networks. For best compatibility with Mac OS 8.5 and later, as well as
with Windows 98, you should use numbers that look like this: 169.x.y,
where x and y are numbers between 0 and 255. Each computer must
have a different value for x or y. For example, you could assign the
IP addresses 169.254.101.1, 169.254.101.2, and 169.254.101.3, and so on.

In this range of IP addresses, the numbers *169.254* identify your local
network, and the last two numbers of each address uniquely identify
one computer or other device that connects to the network.

When you have decided which IP addresses to assign to the computers **Activating**
on your local network, you're ready to configure the TCP/IP software. **TCP/IP**
You do all the work in the TCP/IP control panel, which you'll notice
looks a lot like the AppleTalk control panel with a few more settings.
When you open the TCP/IP control panel, it will tell you if TCP/IP is not
currently active:

▼ Open the TCP/IP control panel by choosing Control Panels from
the Apple menu and double-clicking the TCP/IP icon. If the TCP/IP
system software is inactive, you'll see an alert box asking if you
want to make TCP/IP active so that your TCP/IP configuration will
take effect. Click the Yes button.

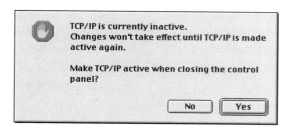

You won't see the alert box if some other program has already activated TCP/IP. For example, TCP/IP is activated when you set up your Mac for Internet access. Once TCP/IP is activated on your computers, it remains active unless you make some effort to render it inactive.

Creating a New Configuration

Rather than changing the existing configuration of the TCP/IP control panel, you should create and save a new configuration expressly for your local network connection. Keep the existing configuration; you may need to use it for a different TCP/IP connection, such as an Internet connection via modem.

To make a new TCP/IP configuration:

1. The TCP/IP control panel should still be open. If it's not, open it now.

2. Choose Configurations from the File menu. The Configurations dialog box (shown below) appears. If more than one configuration is listed on the left side of the dialog box, it doesn't matter which one is selected because you're going to create a new configuration.

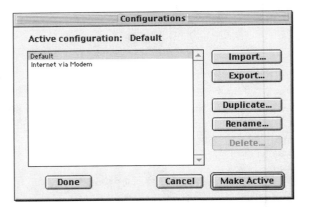

Before the Configurations dialog box appears, you may see an alert box asking if you want to save the changes. This happens only if you made changes to the TCP/IP control panel before choosing Configurations from the File menu. Decide whether you want to save changes, and click the appropriate button in the alert box to carry out your decision.

3. Click the Duplicate button.

4. In the Duplicate Configuration dialog box (shown below), type a descriptive name for the new configuration, such as *Local Network* or *LAN*. Click OK to close this dialog box and return to the Configurations dialog box.

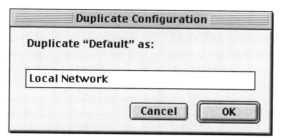

LAN *stands for* **local area network**— *a network of computers in one location, such as a home or small office.*

5. Click the Make Active button to close the Configurations dialog box and return to the TCP/IP control panel.

You have created a new configuration by duplicating an existing configuration. The name you assigned to the new configuration (step 4) appears in the title bar of the TCP/IP control panel.

Changing the Name of a Configuration: If you need to, you can change the name of an existing TCP/IP configuration. From the File menu, choose Configurations (or press Command-K), and then select the configuration you want to rename from the list on the left side of the control panel. Click the Rename button, and edit the name.

The settings for your new TCP/IP configuration may not be correct for your local network. These settings are inherited from the configuration that you duplicated in order to make the new one. You may need to change the Connect Via setting, enter an IP address, and make other changes. Let's take a look at those settings.

Selecting the TCP/IP Port

At the top of the TCP/IP control panel, you need to set up the TCP/IP software to communicate via the port into which the network cable is connected.

1. The TCP/IP control panel should still be open. If it's not, open it now.

The TCP/IP protocol may use the same port as the AppleTalk protocol, or it may use a different one.

2. Click the Connect Via pop-up menu at the top of the control panel, and choose the port that the Mac should use for TCP/IP communications on your local network.

   - If your network cable plugs into the Mac's built-in Ethernet connector, the correct choice is **Ethernet**.

   - **Ethernet** may also be the correct choice if your network plugs into an internal Ethernet adapter card, or the adapter may be listed separately in the Connect Via pop-up menu.

   - If your network plugs into a PC card on a PowerBook, the correct choice is generally **Alternate Ethernet**.

   - If your network plugs into a LocalTalk connector that's attached to the Mac's printer port, the correct choice for the Connect Via setting in the TCP/IP control panel is **AppleTalk (MacIP)**. This causes the TCP/IP protocol to be encapsulated within the AppleTalk protocol and carried on the LocalTalk network hardware connected to the Printer port. The TCP/IP protocol can't be carried directly on LocalTalk hardware.

Specifying an IP Address

Besides choosing a Connect Via setting in the TCP/IP control panel, you need to specify how the Mac will get its unique IP address, as we discussed earlier in this chapter.

If the Mac uses Mac OS 8.5 or later, the computer can assign itself an IP address. If the Mac is running Mac OS 8.1 or earlier, you must enter its IP address manually. (You can also enter an IP address manually in Mac OS 8.5 and later versions, if you prefer.)

Setting a Mac with Mac OS 8.5–8.6 to assign itself an IP address will cause some undesirable side effects. For one, the Mac will lock up for about 10 seconds while assigning itself an IP address. (During this time, the Mac is checking to see whether a DHCP server is available on the network, as discussed in Chapter 5, "Share an Internet Connection.") In addition, the Mac will assign itself a different IP address every five minutes. Together, these two problems mean the Mac will lock up for about 10 seconds every five minutes! What's more, other computers on the network may have trouble staying in contact with a Mac that's changing its IP address so frequently. These problems occur only in Mac OS 8.5–8.6.

To have Mac OS 8.5 or later assign itself an IP address:

Automatically
Assign Address

1. If the TCP/IP control panel is not active, open it now.

2. In the Setup section of the TCP/IP control panel, click the Configure pop-up menu and choose Using DHCP Server. Notice that most of the other TCP/IP settings are provided automatically.

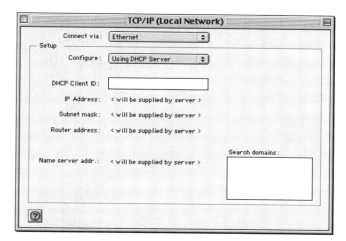

3. You'll see a field called DHCP Client ID. Leave the setting blank. This tells the Mac OS to get an ID from the circuitry that controls the Ethernet connector. If you don't see the DCHP Client ID box, the Mac is not using Mac OS 8.5 or later. You'll have to enter an IP address manually, as described on the next page.

4. Close the TCP/IP control panel.

5. An alert box asks if you want to save the changes you just made. Click the Save button. (This alert does not appear if you did not make any changes before closing the control panel.)

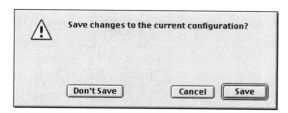

The Mac will assign itself an IP address the next time a program uses the TCP/IP protocol on your network, and the Mac assigns itself a different IP address each time it starts up. The IP address always begins with *169.254* and ends with two numbers randomly selected between 0 and 255. (However, if your network has a DHCP server, the Mac does not assign itself an IP address. In that case, the DHCP server assigns an IP address. See Chapter 5 to learn about DHCP servers.)

Manually Assign Address

To enter an IP address manually:

1. Open the TCP/IP control panel if it's not already open.

2. In the Setup section of the TCP/IP control panel, click the Configure pop-up menu and choose Manually. After you choose this setting, entry fields appear for IP Address, Subnet Mask, Router Address, and Name Server Addr.

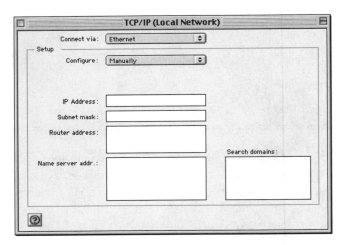

3. In the IP Address field, enter an IP address that begins with *169.254* and ends with two numbers, each between 0 and 255, that you have not assigned to any other computer on your network. Separate the four numbers with periods, similar to what's shown here:

IP Address: 169.254.1.2

4. In the Subnet Mask field, enter *255.255.0.0*. The first two numbers of this IP address identify your local network, and the last two numbers identify a particular machine on the network. The subnet mask gets its name from the fact that it can also be used to divide a network into subnetworks for purposes of IP addressing. The value 255.255.0.0 indicates that your small network has no subnetworks.

Subnet mask: 255.255.0.0

5. In the TCP/IP control panel, leave the Router Address field blank. At this point, your small network has no router. (You'll learn how to add one in Chapter 5.) If numbers appear in this space, delete them.

6. Leave the Name Server Addr. field blank. Name servers are essential on the Internet, but for now your small network will use numeric addresses only. If numbers appear in this space, delete them.

7. Close the TCP/IP control panel.

8. When an alert box asks if you want to save the changes you just made, click the Save button. (This alert does not appear if you did not make any changes before closing the control panel.)

As mentioned earlier in the chapter, the Mac OS allows you to have multiple TCP/IP configurations on each Mac, but you can use only one at a time. For instance, you can use a local network configuration and an Internet configuration, but you can't use the two configurations simultaneously. (However, you can make the Internet available using TCP/IP on your local network, as we discuss in Chapter 5.)

Switching TCP/IP Configurations

If you need to use another configuration, you can easily switch configurations in the TCP/IP control panel. Here's how:

1. Open the TCP/IP control panel.

2. From the File menu, choose Configurations to open the Configurations dialog box (shown earlier in the chapter).

3. In the list on the left side of the dialog box, select the configuration that you want to activate.

4. Click the Make Active button.

5. Close the TCP/IP control panel.

You can also change the TCP/IP configuration using the Location Manager and its Control Strip module or the Control Strip module TCP CC by Tim Kelly (*www.madison-web.com/tkelly/*). The Control Strip and the Location Manager are not installed with Mac OS 8.1 and earlier.

Summary

After hooking up a local network to your Mac, you need to configure the Mac network software. Let's review the main points covered in this chapter:

▼ We recommend that you use the second generation of Mac networking system software, **Open Transport**, which is included with recent Mac OS versions and is available to download free from the Internet (*www.info.apple.com/swupdates/*).

▼ Macs can use multiple network **protocols**, including AppleTalk and TCP/IP. AppleTalk is easier for you to use, but TCP/IP is a faster protocol.

▼ Macs generally use the **AppleTalk** protocol for sharing printers, sharing files, and for many other network services that involve only Macs.

▼ With a little more effort on your part, Macs can also use **TCP/IP** for sharing files and some printers. In addition, Macs, PCs, and other computers can all use the TCP/IP protocol to share an Internet account and for many cross-platform network services.

▼ **To configure AppleTalk,** you activate AppleTalk from the Chooser or the Control Strip and then select the AppleTalk connector in the AppleTalk control panel. You can give the Mac a name in the File Sharing or Sharing Setup control panel.

▼ **To configure TCP/IP for a local network**, you should create a new configuration in the TCP/IP control panel. Then you need to specify how your network connects to the Mac, and configure the Mac's IP address.

▼ On a small local network using TCP/IP, each computer should have a different **IP address** in the range 169.254.0.0 to 169.254.255.255, where the last two numbers are unique for all computers on the local network. A Mac with Mac OS 8.5 or later can assign itself an address in this range. You must assign an IP address manually to a Mac with Mac OS 8.1 or earlier. All computers on the local network should use the **subnet mask** 255.255.0.0.

▼ You can easily **switch** the TCP/IP control panel settings between your local network configuration and your Internet (or any other) configuration.

Part Two

Work and Play

Share an Internet Connection

One of the benefits of having a local network connecting all your computers is that you don't have to provide a modem and a telephone line to each computer to give it access to the Internet. Instead, all the computers on your local network can share one Internet connection. You set up this shared connection by adding an **Internet gateway** to your network; this can be a piece of hardware or some software running on one of your networked computers.

Whether you choose a hardware or software gateway, you'll be able to connect to the Internet through several means: a single regular modem; a high-speed link such as a cable modem; ISDN (Integrated Services Digital Network); or a digital subscriber line (DSL). Windows and Macintosh computers alike can share the same Internet connection.

In this chapter, we'll examine all four types of connections and find out how gateways work. We'll also take a look at some popular choices of the hardware and software gateways that are available to hook up your shared Internet connection.

What Does the Gateway Do?

Before we move on, you should understand generally how an Internet gateway works. As you'd expect by its name, the Internet **gateway** serves as your network's means of controlling access to the Internet. Like a "mailroom in a box," a gateway receives all outgoing communications from the computers on your network and sends them to sites on the Internet via a single connection. The gateway also receives all incoming communications from the Internet and distributes each communication to the correct computer on your local network. All this rerouting is invisible to you and the computers on your network as well as to the computers of the Internet.

We'll explore the details of gateway features and functions later in this chapter, but first let's look into the Internet connection that your network is going to share.

Choosing an Internet Connection

Before you go about deciding whether you want gateway hardware or software for sharing an Internet connection, you should determine the type of connection you want to share: a regular modem, a cable modem, ISDN, or DSL. Let's see how these alternatives compare in terms of performance, cost, convenience, and availability.

Connecting via Regular Modem

For some small networks, an Internet connection via a **single ordinary 56K modem** is an acceptable compromise between cost on one hand and performance and convenience on the other. You can get an Internet account that provides a modem connection from almost any Internet service provider (ISP). Prices are highly competitive because modems and modem accounts are so widely available.

A modem Internet connection can be as inexpensive as you want. It costs less up front than other types of Internet connections (in account setup fees and the cost of the modem), and it costs less month-to-month (for ISP service charges). ISPs generally charge less for setup and monthly usage for a modem connection than they charge for other types of Internet connections.

Cost

Using low-cost modems means you'll have to wait for a dial-up Internet connection.

A modem connection is inexpensive partly because it is active only when someone is using the Internet. To make a connection to the ISP and Internet, your modem must dial up and connect to the ISP's modem and then send the ISP your account name and password.

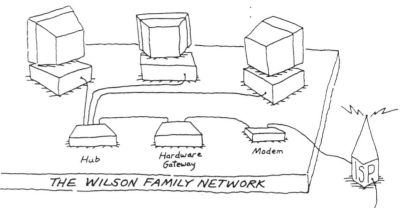

Hub   Hardware Gateway   Modem

THE WILSON FAMILY NETWORK

This dial-up and authentication process can take as long as 30 seconds—a long time to wait every time you want to use the Internet.

If several people want to use the network Internet connection at the same time, only the first person to connect must wait through the dial-up and authentication process. After a connection is established, anyone on the network can access it without waiting. After the last person finishes accessing the Internet, the connection is broken and the modem is idle.

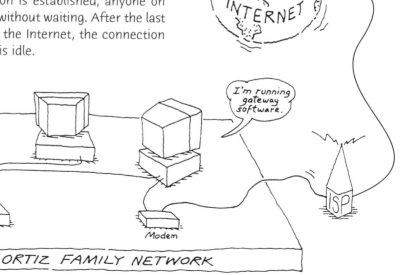

I'm running gateway software.

Hub   Modem

THE ORTIZ FAMILY NETWORK

Speed

A regular modem connection is pretty slow...

Today's fastest modems can receive information at 56.6Kbps (kilobits per second), although it's not unusual for a 56K modem to reduce its speed significantly to maintain a reliable connection on a noisy phone line. What's more, a 56K modem is limited to 33.6Kbps for outgoing data; faster speeds are possible only for incoming data.

...and it's even slower when you share it.

Although a modem connection to the Internet may function fast enough for one computer connection, that's not the case for a network. As the computers on a network access the same modem connection at the same time, everybody's access will become noticeably and ruefully slower. If yours is the only computer connected to the Internet, you'll get access to the modem's entire 56.6Kbps (or whatever your modem can manage, given the quality of your phone line). But after a second person connects to the Internet via the same modem, you have to share that 56.6Kbps. If five people simultaneously engage in high-traffic activities such as downloading files or visiting Web sites, everyone gets an average of 11.2Kbps from the single modem, which is pretty pokey.

Sharing a modem with others is like sharing water with the other members of your household: When everyone in the family turns on a faucet at the same time in a house with small water pipes, every faucet gets only a trickle. You might not need simultaneous access to the Web very often, but when you do need it, it won't be fun to access only at a trickle on a network with a single modem.

Connecting via Cable Modem

There's no getting around it: Modems can't possibly match the speed of the Internet or a local Ethernet network. Because of its limited speed, a modem can be the bottleneck in your Internet connection. You can eliminate this bottleneck by acquiring a faster method to access the Internet, such as a **cable modem**. A cable modem connects your local Ethernet network to a cable television coaxial cable, thereby using the speedy cable TV network to connect to the Internet. And, no, you won't be able to watch cable TV shows on your computer!

The term **cable modem** is something of a misnomer. Unlike a regular modem, which modulates and demodulates digital signals to analog sounds for transmission over voice telephone lines and circuits, a cable modem provides an all-digital link from your computers directly to the Internet.

A cable modem has enormous capacity for ferrying data between the Internet and your computers: The cable modem's **theoretical maximum** rate for **incoming** data is 30Mbps (million bits per second). Its best rate for **outgoing** data from your computers to the Internet is somewhat less—10Mbps. Replacing a regular modem with a cable modem is like replacing skinny water pipes in a house with big wide ones. With a cable modem, several computers can connect to the Internet simultaneously, and nobody will suffer a slowdown.

*They're **Really** Fast*

The **actual speed** your cable modem delivers may be less than the theoretical maximum of 30Mbps. If your cable company offers only 1.5Mbps (1536Kbps), for example, its connection to the Internet backbone (main conduit) may be via a 1.5Mbps T1 line. Other companies connect to the Internet backbone via a 45Mbps T3 line and can offer the superfast 30Mbps. (This 30Mbps limit is imposed by current cable-modem technology.)

T for 1 or T for 3?

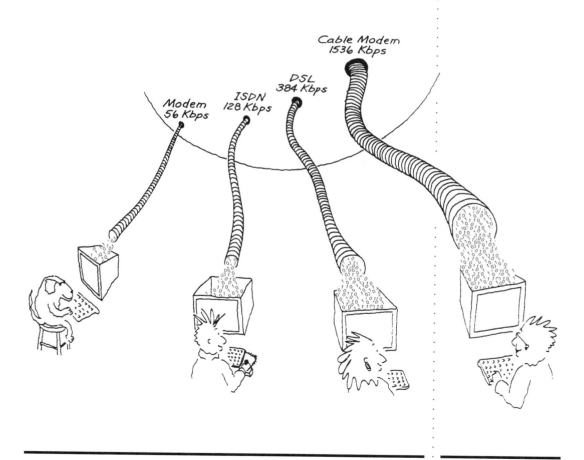

Whatever its nominal rate, 30Mbps or 1.5Mbps, sometimes a cable modem connection to the Internet **does** slow down. Once again, it's similar to the skinny water-pipe problem—when other **homes** in the neighborhood use the Internet through their cable modems at the same time you're doing so, everybody experiences slower service. This happens because all the cable connections in a neighborhood are simultaneously interconnected by the cable that runs down the street to the cable company.

Higher Speed Demands Ethernet

Because the speed of a cable modem would overwhelm the serial port into which an external modem is plugged, cable modems have **Ethernet ports**. A cable modem can be hooked up to a single computer's Ethernet port or to an Ethernet hub used for your network.

Cable Modem Availability

Cable modem service is more often available in residential areas than in business districts.

Unfortunately, superfast cable modem service is not universally available. In the first place, your computer must be located in an area in which cable TV service is available. You might not have this access if your home or office is in a remote location and sometimes if your office is in a business district. Second, the TV cable in your area must be capable of two-way communications. Ordinary cable television service is one-way—TV shows come into your house, but nothing goes out—but cable modem service is a two-way deal. Messages and information come into and out of your network. To accommodate cable modem access in both directions, your cable company will have dedicated a good deal of money and resources to upgrading its system.

Contact your local cable TV provider to see if cable modem service is available in your area.

Cable Equipment Obligations: Don't buy any cable modem equipment before you check with your local cable company. The company may require that you use only certain brands of cable modems; you may even have to buy or rent equipment directly from the cable company.

Cable Modem Pricing

Installing and maintaining a cable modem connection to the Internet costs more than a regular modem connection, but it costs less than the other high-speed connections (ISDN and DSL).

Cable pricing varies from one cable company to another. The company might charge an installation fee and then require that you buy a cable modem from the company. Or it may charge nothing for installation but require that you rent a company-owned cable modem.

On the average, monthly charges for the cable modem connection and Internet services generally run about double what you would pay an ISP for a regular modem account. The monthly fee for cable TV is additional; if you don't want the TV service, you generally pay a higher monthly fee for the modem connection than you'd pay if you wanted TV, too.

Like the cost, the service arrangement varies from one cable company to another. You may deal with a single cable TV company for TV and modem access, or with three different companies providing cable TV, the cable modem connection, and Internet services, respectively. Call your local cable TV company to learn about the arrangement in your area.

Cable Modem Service

If you get cable modem service but don't want cable TV, make sure that the cable company technician installs a **video trap**, which is a filter that prevents you from receiving TV signals. You might think you lucked out if the technician neglects to install the video trap and you're able to watch cable shows for free, but the cable TV company could accuse you of criminal cable fraud! (This has actually happened to people.)

Inside your house or office, the cable attaches to a **splitter box** that includes separate connectors for your cable modem and television. You can plug the cable modem into the uplink port of your network hub using a standard Ethernet cable, or you can plug it into a regular port of the hub using a crossover cable (see Chapter 2).

The Cable Modem Connection

Because a cable modem connection is an Ethernet connection, your computers are always connected to the Internet—no dialing up is required.

Plugging a cable modem into an Ethernet hub makes your local network part of a larger network that includes all your neighbors who also have cable modem connections. Without some protection on your end, those neighbors could potentially access shared files on your computers, and you might be able to access your neighbors' shared files as well. You can protect against this security risk in several ways. For one, you can lock neighbors out of your shared folders and shared disks by requiring a password to connect to a shared item (as explained in Chapter 7).

Cable Modem Security Issues

For more protection, you can install a gateway with a **firewall** that can be set up to filter out file sharing traffic that uses the **TCP/IP protocol** (more on firewalls later in this chapter). TCP/IP is the normal protocol for file sharing in Windows 98 and is an option in Windows 95. Macs mostly use AppleTalk for file sharing but can be set up to use TCP/IP.

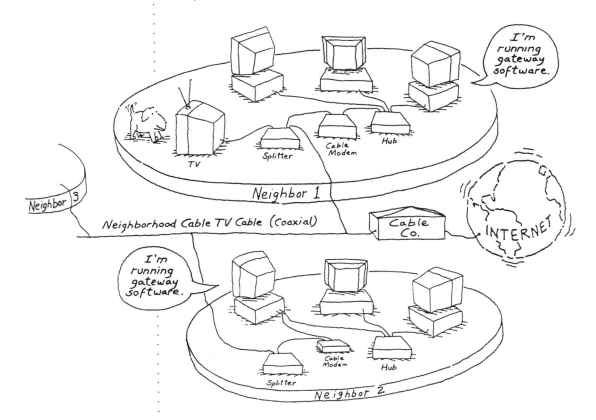

Dual Ethernet Improves Security

You can provide additional security to your local network by plugging the cable modem directly into a gateway that has two Ethernet ports. Your network hub connects to one port, and the cable modem connects to the other. This dual-Ethernet gateway can be a hardware gateway with two Ethernet ports or a software gateway running on a computer that has two Ethernet ports. The gateway provides a path between the ports for Internet traffic and other TCP/IP traffic but does not provide a path for traffic that uses other protocols. For example, the gateway does not provide a path for the NetBEUI protocol, which PCs can use for file and printer sharing, or for the AppleTalk protocol, which most Macs use for file and printer sharing.

Warning to DHCP Users: If your Internet gateway has only one Ethernet port, make sure you don't have a DHCP (Dynamic Host Configuration Protocol) server running on your local network. If you have gateway hardware or software that includes a DHCP server, do not activate the DHCP feature. Do not run separate DHCP server software on any of the computers on your local network. If you do, the DHCP server may try to supply IP addresses to all of your computers on the cable network—including your neighbors' machines! You may be able to restrict your DHCP server to your local network if your Internet gateway has two Ethernet ports; check the DHCP server documentation for details. For more on DHCP servers, see the section "DHCP Servers" later in this chapter and review Chapters 3 and 4.

Using a gateway with two Ethernet ports may also improve Internet performance on the computers in your local network. Because traffic between the gateway and the Internet has its own port, the traffic doesn't have to contend for use of the same port used between the gateway and the local network.

Dual Ethernet means better Internet performance, too.

To help you understand this benefit, imagine you have a mailroom with two doors, In and Out. Each mailroom door is an Ethernet port. Packets of information arrive from the Internet through the In door and go out to the local network through the Out door. If instead of two doors, your mailroom had only one, information heading out to the local network would frequently have to wait for information coming in from the Internet to pass through, and vice versa. As the amount of traffic increases and the single door (the Ethernet port) becomes more congested, the flow of information slows even more.

A cable modem is the most economical high-speed connection to the Internet, but other methods have advantages and may be available in your area if cable is not. **Integrated Signal Digital Network (ISDN)** service, for example, is available via a special dedicated telephone line. Unlike an ordinary phone line, which uses a modem to transmit digital data as analog sounds, an ISDN line transmits digital data only. Because the information is digital, ISDN transmissions flow at a faster rate than those sent via ordinary phone lines and modems.

Connecting via ISDN

ISDN Speed

ISDN: Faster than a regular modem, but slower than cable.

A single ISDN line has two digital channels—**one channel** can transmit data at 64Kbps; **both channels** used simultaneously can transmit data at 128Kbps. (In some areas, the rates are somewhat lower, 56Kbps and 112Kbps, depending on the equipment used by the local telephone company.) These rates are the same for incoming and outgoing data and are not affected by line quality. Thus, ISDN is faster than a regular 56K modem. Against cable modem service, however, ISDN is generally quite a bit slower.

ISDN channels can double as regular phone lines.

In addition to using one or two ISDN channels for data transmission, you can use one or two channels for **voice calls**. For example, you could use one channel to connect to the Internet at 64Kbps (or 56Kbps) and use the other channel to make a phone call. You could use one channel to make a phone call and the other channel to send a fax. Or you could use both channels simultaneously for a 128Kbps (or 112Kbps) Internet connection.

Quick Dial-up Connections

Making an ISDN connection to the Internet is similar to connecting via a regular modem, but the ISDN connection is much quicker. You wait while your computer calls your ISP and establishes a connection. This takes only a couple of seconds, compared with the 15 to 30 seconds using a regular modem. After you're done using the Internet, your computer disconnects.

ISDN Availability

Although not as widely used as regular modem connections to the Internet, ISDN is available in some areas where cable modem service is not. Check with the companies that provide Internet service in your area, and ask if they handle ISDN connections. These companies can tell you how to get an ISDN line, and they might even arrange the installation for you.

Choosing a Provider

The most likely **ISDN provider** is your local phone company, but in some areas other companies provide this service. You might find that your phone company can provide your Internet service or, conversely, the company that provides your Internet service can arrange for the installation of your ISDN line. Doing business with one company is convenient, but you might get a better package of Internet services or pay less overall by dealing separately with your phone company for the ISDN line and with another company for your Internet account.

ISDN Pricing

The cost of ISDN access to the Internet varies widely. In general, ISDN costs more to install and more per month than a regular phone line costs, and an ISDN account may exceed the cost of cable modem service.

Some of the cost depends on how much you use the ISDN line, because you typically pay per minute for each ISDN channel (like a toll call on the telephone). If your network users spend a lot of time on the Internet, the per-minute charges can really add up.

The least expensive way to add ISDN service to a small network is to connect an **ISDN adapter**, commonly called an **ISDN modem**, to one computer and run gateway software on that computer. The ISDN modem can be an external box that plugs into the computer's serial port, or it can be an adapter card similar to an internal modem. The ISDN modem may have one or two phone jacks for a telephone, fax machine, and/or fax modem.

The ISDN Connection

It's also possible to get a hardware gateway with an ISDN adapter built in or with a serial port for connecting a separate ISDN modem. A hardware gateway costs more than a software gateway, but it doesn't require that you leave a computer running and it's more reliable than a computer.

More on gateways later in this chapter.

With an ISDN connection, you don't have to be concerned about isolating your local network from your neighbors or the Internet. Your ISDN modem does not plug into the network hub, so all traffic that flows between your local network and the ISDN connection must go through a gateway. The gateway keeps unauthorized Internet traffic out of your local network and keeps local network traffic private.

A newer telephone-based alternative for Internet connections is **DSL (digital subscriber line)**. There are several varieties of DSL.

Connecting via DSL

The most popular DSL setup for homes and small offices is **ADSL (asymmetric DSL)**. With asymmetric DSL, information coming from the Internet travels faster than data traveling from your local network to the Internet. The specific data rates for an ADSL connection vary by provider, with faster connections inevitably costing more than slower connections. A typical connection for homes and small offices delivers 384Kbps incoming and 128Kbps outgoing. Top speed for ADSL is 8Mbps incoming and 1Mbps outgoing. Faster variants of DSL, such as **SDSL (symmetric DSL)**, are also available at higher cost.

*Variants of DSL are collectively called **xDSL**, or simply DSL.*

DSL signals travel through a regular phone line—in many cases, the same phone line you use every day for phone calls. With DSL installed, you can still use the line for regular phone calls, because DSL transmits its signals at frequencies higher than those of regular calls. (Think dog whistle.) Incredibly, you can make regular telephone calls while simultaneously maintaining a full-speed connection to the Internet!

Simultaneous Phone Calls and Internet Connection

Comparison to ISDN

The DSL connection is better than ISDN, which can maintain only a half-speed connection (on one channel) when you make a phone call (on the other channel). Of course, with a regular modem, you can either make a phone call or connect to the Internet—but you can't do both at the same time, as you can with DSL.

DSL Availability

Although DSL service uses common phone lines, it isn't available everywhere you see a telephone. The service is generally available within three miles of each phone company's central office that has the necessary special equipment installed to provide DSL service. (That central office is the connection point for the phone lines in your vicinity.) Obviously, your local phone company can use its own central offices to install the DSL equipment but so can other companies that want to provide DSL service. Local phone companies tend to offer DSL at lower cost than independent DSL providers, but the independents typically offer faster connections.

DSL Hardware

The type of hardware you'll need for a DSL resembles the hardware for a cable modem connection. Your DSL provider will install a hardware box called a **splitter** that separates your regular phone calls from your Internet connection data. A **DSL modem** plugs into the splitter. Most DSL providers require that you rent or buy the DSL modem from them.

You can connect the DSL modem to your network hub. This does not pose the same security risk as plugging a cable modem into a hub, because your DSL connection is private. (Recall from earlier in this chapter that a cable modem connection makes your local network part of a larger network that could include your neighbors.) Alternatively, instead of plugging the DSL modem into the hub, you can plug it *and* the hub into a dual-Ethernet gateway. Giving the gateway separate connections to the Internet (via the DSL modem) and to your local network (via the hub) reduces congestion between your network and the Internet.

A DSL link is *always* connected to the Internet. There's no waiting to get connected.

Now that you know about the different types of Internet connections that you can share on a local network, you're ready to establish an Internet account with an ISP. The type of connection is just one of many details you need to consider when comparing accounts offered by various ISPs. Let's take a look at the following issues pertaining specifically to sharing an Internet connection on a local network:

- Account sharing
- Public and private IP addresses
- Multiple public addresses
- E-mail addresses

> **Don't Overlook Your Current ISP**: If one of the computers on your network already has its own Internet connection through an ISP—even if it's a regular modem connection and you want a faster connection to share—be sure to investigate the possibility of sharing the existing connection or getting a faster one with the same ISP. Keep in mind that if you stay with your current ISP, your e-mail address won't change, as it might if you switched to another provider.

Establishing an Internet Account

As you study the types of accounts available with each ISP you're considering, keep in mind that you don't need a separate account or a separate connection for each computer on your network. **One account and one connection** for your entire network will do.

One Account, One Connection

> When you tell the ISP you're planning to share the account among all the machines on your network—and you should be up front about your intentions—the ISP may insist that you need a separate account for each computer or one account with separate connections for each computer. If you encounter an ISP that insists on this, forget that ISP and talk to others.

The one Internet connection that you're going to share on your network must have a unique **public IP address** that's different from all other IP addresses on the Internet. Your ISP provides this unique address from among many that are registered to your ISP by the Internet Corporation for Assigned Names and Numbers (ICANN).

One Public IP Address

You'll need only one public IP address for your entire local network. The hardware or software gateway that you install enables all the computers on your network to use the same public IP address simultaneously, as explained later in the section "About Internet Gateways."

Private IP Addresses

The individual computers on your network use the public IP address only for Internet communications. To communicate within the local network, each computer uses the **private IP address** it was assigned when you set up its network software in Chapter 3 (Windows) or 4 (Macintosh).

Private IP addresses can't be used on the Internet because they are taken from a range of IP addresses officially designated for private local networks. All local networks are free to use this range of IP addresses privately; if the same range were used by all networks on the Internet, however, there would be many instances of address duplication. Only one Internet address can be assigned for each connection, worldwide.

Multiple Public IP Addresses

Although you need only one public IP address for your entire network—and that's all you'll get with the least expensive Internet account—you may decide to sign up for an Internet account that bundles multiple IP addresses with other features. In this case, your network can simply share one of your public IP addresses, and each computer on your local network can continue to use the private IP address that you already assigned it. Alternatively, you could replace each computer's private IP address with a different public IP address from the group of public IP addresses assigned by your ISP. If you choose to use the public IP addresses instead of private IP addresses on your network, your ISP should help you set up each computer.

Dynamic vs. Static IP Addresses: With some types of Internet accounts, you won't use the same public IP address every time you connect, because the ISP dynamically assigns addresses from a pool of reusable addresses. This type of address is called a **dynamic IP address**. It's fine to use for most small networks. But if you ever decide to serve Web pages or provide other services to the Internet from any of your computers, your ISP will need to assign you a **static IP address**—one that doesn't change—so Internet users can find your site.

Many E-mail Addresses

Although you need only one Internet account, one Internet connection, and one public IP address for your entire network, everyone who sends and receives e-mail via the Internet will want a separate e-mail address. Most ISPs will add e-mail addresses to an account for a small monthly charge per address. This is far less expensive than paying for an entirely separate account for each networked computer.

The issues raised here with respect to sharing an Internet account are certainly not the only questions you must consider when selecting an ISP and an Internet account. For example, you must also balance the cost of the account with the features it includes. Pay attention to how easily (or with what difficulty!) you can get technical support. Of course, you need to make sure the ISP supports the kinds of computers you have on your network (some ISPs don't support Macs, for example).

> The ISP should provide instructions and assistance for setting up an account and getting it working on one machine. But don't expect the ISP to help you arrange the computers on your local network so they can share your single Internet account. You'll need to select and install an Internet gateway to do that.

Other ISP Issues

In addition to finding an ISP to provide the type of Internet connection you want, you need to decide how you're going to make the Internet account available to all the computers on your local network. Basically, you have to choose between a **hardware gateway** and a **software gateway**. If you're using an Ethernet network, you can plug a free-standing hardware gateway into your Ethernet hub, just as you plugged in your computers. Alternatively, you can run software on one of your networked computers to perform the same function as the hardware gateway.

About Internet Gateways

> **Gateway Name Game:** Internet gateways, both hardware and software, go by various names. Some are called Internet **gateways**, others Internet **routers**, and still others are called **proxy servers**. Technically speaking, routers, gateways, and proxy servers are different animals, but manufacturers use the terms loosely.

Hardware gateways and software gateways have a common set of features, but individual gateway products rarely include every feature available. Let's investigate the bells and whistles you'll encounter on gateway products to help you determine which ones are important for your network. Later, we'll look at some representative hardware and software gateways.

At the heart of every gateway is some means of directing traffic traveling between the Internet and your networked computers. The Internet delivers everything destined for your network computers to your gateway, and the gateway sees to it that each incoming packet goes to the appropriate computer on your network. When your networked

Traffic Director

computers send data to the Internet, your gateway takes the outgoing packets off the local network and forwards them through the shared Internet connection. The gateway's actions are transparent to people using the Internet from your network's computers.

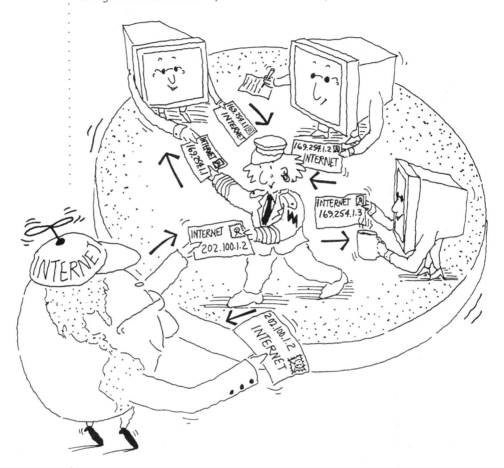

Network Address Translation (NAT)
Some gateways direct traffic between your local network and the Internet by hiding the network's private IP addresses behind the single public IP address provided by your ISP. The Internet gateway translates the private IP addresses to one public IP address for outgoing Internet traffic and routes all information requests from your local network to the Internet using the public IP address. When information is returned from the Internet, the gateway translates and forwards incoming Internet traffic from your public IP address to the appropriate private IP address of the destination computer that requested information.

This process is called **network address translation (NAT)**. It's also called **IP masquerading**, because all your networked computers masquerade as one computer on the Internet (because they share an IP address).

Other Internet gateways direct traffic between your network and the Internet by mediating communications among servers on the Internet and client applications on your local networked computers. The gateway has a **proxy server**, which acts as a go-between for your network and for the servers on the Internet.

Proxy Servers

Instead of requesting Web pages, e-mail service, and other Internet services directly, all your networked computers request the services from the gateway's proxy server. The proxy server then forwards the requests to the actual Internet servers on behalf of your networked computers. The Internet servers send the Web page requests, e-mail, and so forth to the proxy server, and it forwards the materials to the appropriate computers on your local network.

Since your networked computers contact only the proxy server, you may need to set up each machine's Web browser, e-mail software, and other Internet applications so that they look to the proxy server for Internet services.

Setting Up for the Proxy Server

Internet applications on your networked computers generally need to be set up to use the gateway's proxy server.

Browsers: You must set the Web browser preferences or options on all your computers to use the proxy server instead of going directly to the Internet.

E-mail: You must set up the proxy server with the name of your ISP's SMTP server for outgoing mail (for example, mail.domainname.com) and the name of your ISP's POP3 server for incoming mail (for example, pop.domainname.com). If your ISP provides an IMAP 4 server for improved handling of incoming mail, you should specify it as well (for example, imap4.domainname.com). In addition, you need to set up your e-mail program, such as Microsoft Outlook or Qualcomm Eudora, to use the proxy server instead of the ISP's SMTP, POP3, and IMAP 4 servers.

Other Internet Applications: You may discover that a particular Internet application can't be set to use a proxy server. You won't be able to use this application with a *shared* Internet connection; instead, you'd use the application only on a computer with its *own* Internet connection. Conversely, you may discover that a particular proxy server doesn't

A few applications for the Internet don't work through a proxy server, and some proxy servers don't handle particular Internet services.

support an Internet service that one of your applications uses (for example, a service used for multiplayer gaming over the Internet). An application like this would run only on a computer with its own Internet connection.

The Gateway Cache

A software gateway may also include a **cache**, which stores Web pages that the gateway has received from Internet servers. Once a page is stored in the cache, the gateway can send it to a requesting computer on your network without having to access the Internet. This increases the apparent responsiveness of the Internet for Web users on the network.

Some gateways download frequently-used Web pages even before being asked for them and store them in the cache. No, the gateway isn't clairvoyant—it just keeps track of the most frequently used Web pages and downloads them in advance so you don't have to wait.

Security on Gateways

Most software and hardware gateways come equipped with security measures that prevent unauthorized people (hackers) from breaking into your networked computers from the Internet.

Firewalls

Either a proxy server or NAT (IP masquerading) can serve as a **firewall** that provides security for your network by blocking access for unsolicited Internet traffic.

*A **firewall** protects your local network from a potentially untrustworthy network, such as the Internet.*

Here's how it works: A computer on the Internet cannot directly contact your network's computers because it doesn't know your computers' private IP addresses. Computers on the Internet can access only the public IP address of your gateway. The firewall gateway ignores incoming Internet traffic unless it is sent to your public IP address specifically in response to outgoing traffic generated by one of your network computers.

In addition to blocking unsolicited Internet traffic, some firewalls can be configured to filter out TCP/IP traffic from specific applications. For instance, you could set up such a firewall to filter out all file sharing and printer sharing that uses the TCP/IP protocol. This would prevent anyone on the Internet from accessing shared items on your local network. If you have a cable modem connection and your computers use TCP/IP for file sharing and printer sharing, the firewall could also prevent neighbors with cable modems from accessing your shared items.The firewall feature of an Internet gateway does not block any network traffic that uses a protocol other than TCP/IP, however.

Windows can use the TCP/IP or NetBEUI protocol for file and printer sharing, and Mac OS file sharing and printing normally uses the AppleTalk protocol. As mentioned earlier, an Internet gateway with two Ethernet ports will keep your NetBEUI and AppleTalk file and printer sharing private from your cable modem neighbors.

Other features in your Internet gateway can add even more security. Some software gateways include **authentication**. Authentication works by requiring each person on your network to supply a valid ID and password to access the Internet. In addition, you can set up some software gateways to restrict particular Internet services or certain Internet locations. For example, a gateway could allow some people to send and receive e-mail but not surf the Web; or a gateway could limit access to Web sites you deem undesirable.

Authentication and Other Preventives

Some Internet gateways include a **DHCP server**, which automatically assigns IP addresses to each of the computers on your local network. This saves you the trouble of manually assigning IP addresses. Of course, you must set up each computer on your network to automatically request its IP address from the DHCP server. A PC will make this request each time you start it up, and a Mac will request the first time you use an application that requires the TCP/IP protocol, such as a Web browser or an e-mail program.

DHCP Servers

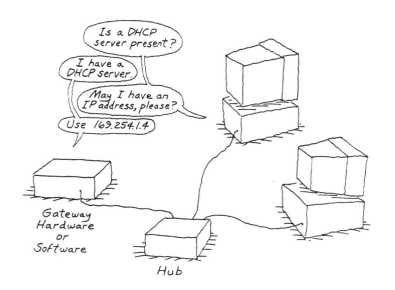

To set up automatic IP addressing in Windows:

1. In the Control Panel, double-click the Network icon.

2. Double-click the TCP/IP protocol listing for the computer's network adapter, and select Obtain an IP Address Automatically in the IP Addressing tab.

(For detailed instructions, review Chapter 3.)

To set up DHCP addressing on a Mac:

1. Open the TCP/IP control panel, and choose Configurations from the File menu.

2. Double-click the name of the configuration for your local network, and choose Using DHCP Server from the Configure pop-up menu.

(Review Chapter 4 for detailed instructions.)

Hardware Gateways

Today, lots of **hardware Internet gateways** are available with a wide range of features and prices. Hardware gateways have several advantages over software gateways, but you have to pay a higher price to get the advantages—hardware gateways cost more because they're self-sufficient. Unlike its software cousin, the hardware gateway doesn't require that a computer be turned on to provide an Internet connection for your network. A hardware gateway is also more reliable; it isn't nearly as susceptible to crashing as a software gateway's computer.

A hardware gateway can't use a networked computer's internal modem.

A hardware gateway's self-sufficiency means it can't use a computer's internal modem to connect to the Internet. If you want to share a regular modem connection to the Internet with other networked computers, your hardware gateway must have its own modem. Some hardware gateways offer built-in modems or ISDN modems, and some have serial ports for external modems or ISDN modems. Others have an Ethernet port for connecting a cable modem or DSL modem.

Following are product profiles for some hardware gateways that are available for a home or small office network.

Netopia's Line

Netopia offers a line of hardware Internet gateways for small networks. One model includes two internal modems and a serial port for a third external modem. If your ISP supports a feature called **multilink PPP (Multilink Point-to-Point Protocol)**, you can combine two 56K modems (each on a separate phone line) for a single Internet connection at 112Kbps. You can also add a third modem for a connection speed of 168Kbps. (You'll find other products that support the multilink PPP feature as well.)

Other Netopia models work with ISDN, cable modem, and DSL connections to the Internet. Netopia gateways include a DHCP server, and some have an integrated eight-port 10BaseT hub. For information, go to *www.netopia.com*.

The multilink PPP technology allows you to create a virtual link with more capacity than a single physical link.

The **WebRamp** line of Internet gateways is a diverse group of integrated office devices. Some have three serial ports for external modems or ISDN modems; others include built-in modems or ISDN modems. Some include fax software, and some have built-in Ethernet hubs.

WebRamp Line from Ramp Networks

The WebRamp gateways can use multilink PPP if your ISP supports it. If not, WebRamp products can use a proprietary scheme for combining two or three modems on separate phone lines to get a faster Internet connection. But be careful here and don't go overboard, or you may end up paying for gateway features you don't need—such as the ability to connect to a WAN (wide area network), support of IPX routing, or support of Windows NT Virtual Private Networking. For information about these gateway products, visit Ramp Networks at *www.rampnet.com*.

The **InBusiness Internet Station from Intel** offers three places to plug in a modem or an ISDN modem: a serial port and two PC card slots. InBusiness uses any one of these points for sharing an Internet connection on your local network. An additional two fax modems can be shared by all the PCs on your network for faxing or connecting to online services, just as though the shared modem were connected to the network PC. If your local network includes Macs, they can share the Internet connection but can't share the other two modems.

Intel's InBusiness Internet Station

The Intel gateway doesn't offer some of the features of Netopia and WebRamp gateways, such as multilink PPP. For more information, see *www.intel.com/network/products/inbusiness_internet.htm*.

The **ProxyServer gateways from Multi-Tech Systems** do not actually use a proxy server for Internet sharing. Like the other hardware gateways profiled here, the Multi-Tech gateways use NAT (IP masquerading) for Internet sharing. One Multi-Tech gateway model has a serial port for sharing an Internet connection via an external modem or an ISDN modem. Another model has three built-in 56K modems and supports multilink PPP for a connection at up to 168Kbps. You can also get a model for connecting to the Internet via cable modem or DSL.

Multi-Tech's Internet ProxyServer

For more on this gateway product, see *www.multitech.com/products/*.

Software Gateways

As an alternative to a hardware gateway, you can install a software gateway on one of your computers. Gateway software is available for both Windows and Macintosh computers. All gateway software can handle Internet traffic for both platforms, regardless of the type of computer on which the software has been installed.

Software gateways cost less but have drawbacks.

Gateway software generally costs less than its hardware counterparts with similar features, but using the software can have a few drawbacks. The computer running a software gateway **must remain turned on** while anyone on the network seeks access to the Internet. Obviously, if this computer crashes, everyone on the network loses Internet connection until the gateway software and host machine can be restarted. If this arrangement is acceptable for your network, you can save money by opting for the software solution.

Another disadvantage: If a user is downloading a large file through a software gateway running on another PC, you'll probably notice some effect on that computer—that is, the machine running the software gateway will slow down. (Of course, you can always choose to install the software on a dedicated machine, but there go your savings....)

A Sampling of What's Available

Dozens of good Internet gateway software products offer the features we've described so far in this chapter. The following product profiles represent only a bit of what's available. All of these products are popular and have garnered good reviews. Unless otherwise noted, they support Internet connections via modem as well as high-speed connections via ISDN, cable modem, and DSL. Like many other applications, you can download free time-limited versions of these gateway packages from their respective Web sites and try them out.

WinGate from Deerfield.Com

WinGate from Deerfield.Com runs on Windows 95, Windows 98, or Windows NT. Its main feature is a proxy server that provides Web, FTP, and e-mail access for all the computers on your network. WinGate includes an integrated DHCP server that automatically assigns IP addresses to your computers. It also offers an auditing feature that will record what sites and services are being accessed by users.

WinGate comes with a simple installation program. It runs as a Windows service, which means that it starts when Windows starts. Users don't have to log in—they can access the Internet at any time. For more information, see the WinGate demo at *www.wingate.com*.

Both **Vicomsoft Internet Gateway** and **Vicomsoft SoftRouter Plus** are available for Windows and Macintosh computers. Both use the NAT process to share an Internet connection. They will also work with a hardware router, should you want to add one later. Other features include a DHCP server for automated IP addressing , a Web cache, and a remote access server to let you connect to your local network from the outside.

Vicomsoft Products

Both products are easy to install and set up. The Vicomsoft Internet Gateway product costs more than the Vicomsoft SoftRouter Plus because the former comes with a year's subscription to the CyberNOT service, which you can use to block Web pages whose content you deem objectionable. **Vicomsoft SurfDoubler** is essentially the same product as Vicomsoft SoftRouter Plus, but it allows only two computers to connect to the Internet at a time and it is available for Macintosh only.

You can download demo versions from *www.vicomsoft.com.*

WinProxy from Ositis Software is a proxy server for Windows computers. It includes a DNS server and support for most Internet protocols, and it allows connection to America Online through the proxy server. This software does not include a DHCP server; you must manually enter the IP address for each computer on your local network.

Ositis Software's WinProxy

You can see a demo version at *www.winproxy.com.*

The shareware **WinProxy** software from LAN Projekt is another proxy server for use on Windows computers. WinProxy is easy to set up and can be configured to cache frequently accessed sites to speed up response time.

LAN Projekt's WinProxy

You can install the software from *www.lanprojekt.cz/winproxy/.*

IPNetRouter from Sustainable Softworks is software gateway for Macintosh. It does network address translation and includes a DHCP server.

Sustainable Softworks' IPNetRouter

An IPNetRouter demo is available at *www.sustworks.com.*

Summary

The ability to share an Internet link with all of your networked computers is another compelling reason to set up a network. It can save you money and provide the access everyone needs to the Web, e-mail, and other Internet services.

▼ For some small networks, an Internet connection via a single ordinary **56K modem** is an acceptable compromise between cost and performance.

▼ A **cable modem** connection to the Internet is faster than a regular modem but isn't available everywhere. It also costs more and may slow down if several of your neighbors use the same cable company and start using cable modems on their computers.

▼ An **ISDN** connection to the Internet is faster than a regular modem but not nearly as fast as a cable modem. ISDN can be expensive.

▼ A **DSL** connection is considerably faster than ISDN or a regular modem, but a cable modem can be faster. Like cable modems, DSL is always connected to the Internet—no dial-up is involved.

▼ You need only one **Internet account** with an ISP, and you need only one **public IP address** from the ISP. But you will probably want multiple **e-mail addresses** to accommodate all of your networked computers and users.

▼ An **Internet gateway,** whether hardware or software, directs traffic between your network and the Internet. The gateway may use the network address translation (NAT) process, also known as IP masquerading, or it may include a proxy server that does the job.

▼ A gateway may **cache** Web pages for immediate local redistribution to computers on your network, saving you the time of fetching them from the Internet again.

▼ A gateway may include a **DHCP server**, which automatically assigns IP addresses to your network computers so you don't have to do it manually.

▼ **Hardware gateways** incorporate gateway features in various combinations and are available from many manufacturers.

▼ Dozens of **software gateways** offer the gateway features described in this chapter.

Share Printers

6

The desire to share a high-end printer among several computers is reason enough to install a network. Printing over a network is a lot like printing to a printer connected directly to your computer. But before you can use a shared printer, you'll need to install and configure some software.

As with other aspects of networking, sharing a printer among Macintosh computers is quite a bit different from sharing among Windows machines. In some cases, however, you can set up a network so that both PCs and Macs can use the same printer.

Types of Printers to Share

On a network, you can share just about any type of printer, from an inexpensive inkjet to a big, fancy, feature-filled laser printer. Some printers are designed to connect directly to an Ethernet or LocalTalk network; these **network printers** are made specifically for sharing. But you can also share many of the **local printers**, also known as **personal printers**, that directly connect to one of the computers on the network. Where a printer is connected to the network affects how you set it up for sharing but not how you print to it. We'll detail all these procedures in this chapter.

> **The Local Angle**: A **local network** is the network in your home or office, but a **local printer** is plugged directly into one computer. You can set up your network to share both local and network printers.

Local Printers

Local printers are designed to **connect to one computer**. Most inkjet printers are local printers, as are the older dot-matrix printers that some people still use for printing on carbon-copy paper. Some laser printers are local printers as well.

When you share the local printer connected to your computer, your computer provides the network connection to other computers. Other network computers that want to print to your shared local printer must contact your computer over the network and send your computer the pages to be printed. Your computer has to do a bit of processing before it tells its printer to print the pages. This means your computer must be up and running if anyone wants to use your shared local printer, and it also means that processing some of those printing jobs could cause some minor delays on your machine if you're simultaneously working on your computer as another user is printing.

An independent network printer isn't "local" because it doesn't connect to any single computer. Rather, an independent printer **connects directly to the network,** just like a computer (via a hub, for example). In fact, an independent network printer actually *is* a computer—with a processor and RAM of its own. This additional equipment enables the network printer to communicate directly with the computers on the network.

Independent Network Printers

An independent network printer is always available to all network computers, just as if it were connected directly to each computer. The biggest drawback to this setup, however, is that independent network printers are usually more expensive than local printers.

Many laser printers are independent network printers; most inkjet printers are not.

Ports and Adapters

Independent network printers are easy to identify. Just look for the network port—either a **10BaseT Ethernet** port or a **LocalTalk** port. (Review Chapter 2 for details on Ethernet and LocalTalk.)

*Network adapters made for printers are also called **print servers**.*

If a printer doesn't have a network port, you may be able to add one by installing a **network adapter** card in the printer. Adding an internal or external network adapter essentially turns a local printer into an independent network printer.

To determine whether your printer has an expansion slot for a network adapter, check the printer manual or ask the printer manufacturer. Even if your printer doesn't have an expansion slot for an internal network adapter, you may be able to use an external network adapter to connect the printer to your network. The printer manufacturer may also be able to tell you whether there is an external network adapter that will work with your printer, or you can check with a computer store or catalog.

Mind Your Network Protocol

Some older network printers have only a LocalTalk port—often called an **AppleTalk port** by printer manufacturers, because LocalTalk can use only the AppleTalk protocol. Printers with an Ethernet port can use many network protocols, including AppleTalk and TCP/IP.

AppleTalk is chiefly a Macintosh protocol. PCs can't communicate with network printers that use only the AppleTalk protocol because Windows 95 and 98 don't normally support it. For example, a printer with a LocalTalk port but no Ethernet port can use only AppleTalk.

You can, however, add AppleTalk support to Windows 95 and 98 by installing additional software that's not included with Windows. Alternatively, you may be able to bypass the AppleTalk protocol altogether by connecting the printer to a PC as a local printer. These solutions are all more thoroughly described in "Connecting PCs to AppleTalk Printers" later in this chapter.

Getting Ready to Share a Printer

To share a printer among the computers on your network, that printer needs a **physical connection**—either to one of the network computers if it's a local printer or directly to the network if it's a network printer. Each network computer must have installed the appropriate **driver software** for the printer as well as **network printing software**.

A local printer connects to one of the ports on the back or side of one of your computers. Generally, you connect the printer to the computer using a cable included with the printer. The type of cable depends on whether the printer was made for the PC, Macintosh, or both.

- Most local printers for PCs connect using a **parallel cable**.

- Most local printers for Macs connect with a **serial cable**.

- Newer printers can connect to both PCs and Macs using a **USB cable** (universal serial bus).

We'll explain how to connect a local printer later, in "Connect the Printer to the PC" and "Connect the Printer to the Mac."

> **USB Converters**: If you want to connect a local printer that doesn't have a USB port to a computer that has only USB ports, you may be able to buy a converter cable for the printer. Hewlett-Packard and Epson sell USB converters for their own printers, and other companies also offer converter cables. Check with your local computer store to see what's available.

Like a network computer, an independent network printer connects directly to your network. If you have an Ethernet network, you'll need 10BaseT patch cable long enough to reach a nearby network jack or your Ethernet hub. If you have a LocalTalk network, you'll need a LocalTalk connector and a phone cord. All this equipment is described in Chapter 2.

Network Printer Connection

A network printer may have its own network port, or it may plug into an external network adapter.

> If you've set up an Ethernet network and your network printer has only a LocalTalk port, don't panic. You can get a LocalTalk-to-Ethernet converter. These are described in the later section "Connect a LocalTalk Printer to an Ethernet Network."

Whether you have an independent network printer that connects directly to your network or you will share a local printer that connects to one of your computers, all of your computers must have compatible **driver software** for that printer to use it via the network. The driver software communicates with the printer using a set of commands, a kind of **printer language**. Using the printer language, the driver tells the printer what to print on each page, along with instructions on how many copies to make, what paper tray to use, and which special features of the printer to use.

Drivers and Printer Languages

Printer Control Language

The most common printer language is Hewlett-Packard's **Printer Control Language (PCL)**. It is used in both local and network printers. PCL is found on simple, inexpensive printers as well as complex, high-priced printers.

Another common printer language is **PostScript**, which was created by Adobe Systems. PostScript printers are usually network printers (but not all network printers are PostScript printers). PostScript printers are usually more expensive than PCL printers and can print higher quality graphics. Some network printers support both PCL and PostScript.

PostScript

PostScript printers often give you a choice of driver software to install, including the driver that came with your computer, the driver from the printer manufacturer, or the driver from Adobe.

The **PostScript printer language** is not the same as **PostScript Type 1 fonts**. PostScript Type 1 fonts can be used on non-PostScript printers, provided your computer has the Adobe Type Manager (ATM) software installed. On the other hand, a PostScript printer is not limited to PostScript Type 1 fonts. It can also use **TrueType fonts**, which come with Windows and the Mac OS.

Some local printers use neither PCL nor PostScript; instead, they use proprietary printer languages invented by the printer manufacturer.

Upgrade to PostScript: It's possible to add PostScript capability to some printers that don't have it initially. You generally do this by installing a small adapter card, sometimes called a **PostScript SIMM**, inside the printer.

Network Software

Before it can use printers over the network, each of your computers needs to have network software installed. We assume that you have already set up your network as described in the preceding chapters.

Also, if you want to share a local printer with other computers on your network, you'll need to install additional software to provide network print services, as described next.

With Windows 95 and 98, a local printer attached to one PC can be shared with other PCs on your network. To set this up, you'll need to do the following:

1. Connect the printer to the PC.
2. Install the printer driver software.
3. Install Network File and Print Services.
4. Set the access control.
5. Create a shared printer.

Let's go over these five steps in detail. (If you intend to share a local printer that's already in use on the PC, you can skip the next two sections and go right to "Install Network File and Print Services.")

> A few local printer models can't be shared. If the documentation for your local printer doesn't expressly advise you that your printer can't be shared, go ahead and try sharing it.

The procedure for connecting a local printer to a PC is the same whether you are using it for yourself or sharing it with a network.

- If the printer has a **parallel cable,** just plug one end into the printer. Plug the other end into the PC's parallel port or into the pass-through parallel port of a scanner or other device that's already connected to the PC.

- If the printer has a **USB cable,** plug one end into the printer. Plug the other end into a USB port on the computer or into a USB hub that's connected to the computer.

- If the printer has both a parallel cable and a USB cable, you can use either one.

For specific directions on connecting your local printer to one of your computers, consult the printer's installation instructions.

After connecting a local printer to a PC, the printer's driver software must be installed on the PC and an icon for the printer must be added to the PC's Printers folder. Windows may initiate the process automatically when you restart the PC. If not, you can take care of it using the Add Printer Wizard.

To install driver software and an icon for a printer:

1. Click the Start button, select Settings, and click Printers. The Printers window appears.

   You can also display the Printers window by double-clicking the Printers icon in My Computer or in the Control Panel.

Setting Up a Local PC Printer for Sharing

If you want to set up a shared printer on a Macintosh, skip ahead several pages to "Setting Up a Local Mac Printer for Sharing."

Connect the Printer to the PC

Install the Printer Driver

2. Double-click the Add Printer icon to launch the Add Printer Wizard.

3. Click the Next button to begin.

4. Select Local Printer and click the Next button.

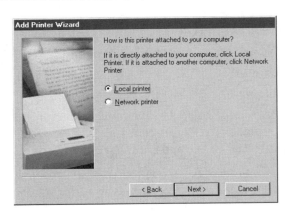

Tell the Add Printer Wizard you are adding a local printer.

5. The Wizard displays lists of printer makes and models, as shown below. Select the name of your printer's manufacturer from the list on the left and your printer model from the list on the right.

If your printer isn't listed, you'll need to provide a disk that contains the printer's driver software:

- Click the Have Disk button. In the dialog box that appears, specify the location of the driver. Then click OK to return to the Add Printer Wizard.

- If Windows asks for the disk you specified, insert it so that the driver software can be copied to the PC's hard disk.

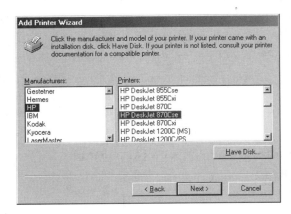

If you don't see the make and model of your printer, click Have Disk.

6. Click the Next button.

7. Select the port that the printer uses. You'll see a list that generally includes COM1, COM2, and LPT1. LPT1 is a typical choice. COM1 and COM2 are often used for modem connections and sometimes for a mouse or graphics tablet connection. Click the Next button.

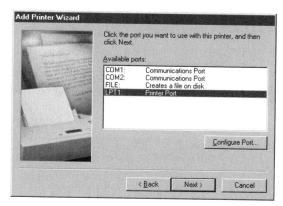

Select the port to which your printer is connected.

8. The Wizard asks whether you want to make this printer your **default printer**—the printer to which many Windows applications will automatically print. Click Yes if this is your only printer or if it's your default printer. Select No if you want to designate another printer as the default. Then click Next.

9. The Wizard asks if you want to print a test page. Click Yes.

Windows may next ask you to insert the Windows Installation CD-ROM (or some of the installation floppies if you have an older copy of Windows). Windows will copy the needed files to your hard drive and then may ask you to restart your computer. Once you've done this, the test page will print to your printer.

Install Network File and Print Services

With the driver for your computer's local printer installed, you can print to the printer from your computer—but it's not available on your network yet. To set this up, you need to install the Windows software that lets other network devices access the local printer connected to your PC (and the folders on your hard drive, which is the subject of the next chapter). You'll do this in the Network dialog box.

To install Microsoft File and Print Services:

1. Open the Control Panel and double-click the Network icon. The Network dialog box appears, with the Configuration tab on top.

2. Click the Add button to open the Select Network Component Type dialog box.

3. Select Service as the type of network component you want to install, and then click Add.

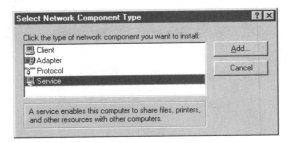

4. At this point, the procedure differs for Windows 98 and Windows 95. Do one of the following:

- **For Windows 98,** a dialog box appears listing several services. Select File and Printer Sharing for Microsoft Networks. Click OK.

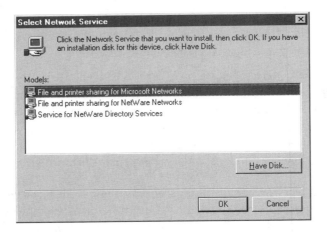

- **For Windows 95,** a dialog box appears with two lists. In the Manufacturers list, select Microsoft; in the Network Services list, select File and Printer Sharing for Microsoft Networks. Click OK.

5. Windows may now ask you to insert your installation CD-ROM so it can copy the printer-sharing files to your hard disk.

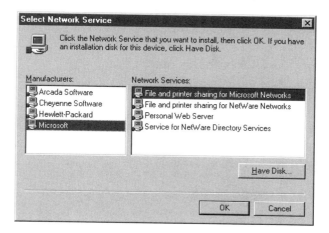

6. Windows once again displays the Configuration tab of the Network dialog box. Scroll the list at the top of the dialog box, and you'll find File and Printer Sharing for Microsoft Networks is now included in this list. Click the button labeled File and Print Sharing.

7. In the File and Print Sharing dialog box that appears, click the check box labeled "I want to be able to allow others to print to my printer(s)" to turn on this setting. (For printer sharing, it doesn't matter whether the other check box is checked or not.) Click OK.

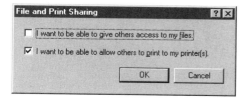

You'll now return to the Configuration tab of the Network dialog box. There's just one more simple thing you need to do—set the access control.

Set the Access Control

Each printer you make available to the network is called a **share**. (The same term applies to folders that you share, as you'll see in Chapter 7.) You now need to tell Windows that you want to control access at the share level. This means you'll be able to set a password for each shared printer (as described in the next section, "Create a Shared Printer").

To set the share-level access control:

1. In the Network dialog box, click the Access Control tab.

2. Select Share-level Access Control, and then click OK.

   You can ignore the other option, the User-level Access Control. It requires that your network have a server computer that stores a list of user names and passwords.

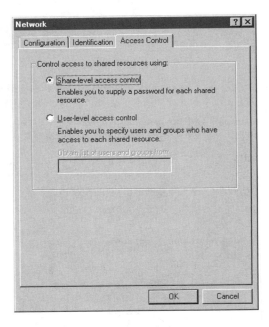

3. At this point, Windows may ask you to insert the Windows Installation CD-ROM (or some of the installation floppies). Windows will copy files to your hard drive and then ask you to restart your computer. You can do this now or push on to create a share.

Create a Shared Printer

The process of enabling others on the network to access a particular printer or folder on your PC is called **creating a share**. You create a printer share from the Printers window, which lists local and network printers available to your computer.

To create a shared printer:

1. Click the Start button, select Settings, and then choose Printers. The Printers window appears.

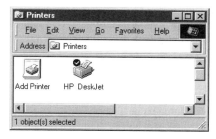

2. Click to select the icon of the local printer you want to share with others.

> With both Windows 95 and 98, you can share only a printer that is plugged into your computer. You can't share any printer whose icon shows a cable connected to the printer—this indicates a network printer.

3. From the File menu, choose Sharing. This opens the printer's Properties dialog box, with the Sharing tab on top. (You can also right-click the printer icon and choose Sharing from the shortcut menu.)

4. Click the Shared As option.

5. In the Share Name field, enter a name for the printer. This name will appear on other network users' machines when they access your computer in their Network Neighborhood.

> In the Comment field, you can type a phrase that describes the printer or its location. If you have more than one printer, this comment will help users identify the printer.

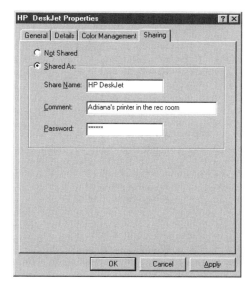

The printer name and comment can be seen by other network users. A password is optional.

6. Type a password, if desired, or just leave the password field blank.

7. Click the OK button.

In the Printers window, you'll notice a picture of a hand below your printer's icon; this indicates that it is a shared printer. (If the printer icon also has a check mark, it means the printer is the default printer for this computer.)

8. Restart Windows.

Setting Up a Local Mac Printer for Sharing

If you want to set up a shared printer in Windows, go back several pages to "Setting Up a Local PC Printer for Sharing."

On a Mac, the local printers you can share over a network are Apple StyleWriter models, the LaserWriter LS, Personal LaserWriter 300, LaserWriter Select 300, and a few others. You'll need to complete the following tasks to share a Mac Printer:

1. Connect the printer to the Mac.

2. Install a Mac printer driver.

3. Share the printer.

Let's go over the steps for these three tasks. (If you're going to share a local printer that's already in use on a Mac, you can skip ahead to "Share the Printer.")

Connect the Printer to the Mac

Your first job is to connect the local printer to the Mac that will share it with other computers on your network. Whether the local printer is used on one computer or shared on a network, you plug it into a Mac in the same way.

- If the printer has a serial cable, just plug one end into the printer. Plug the other end into one of the Mac's serial ports—the Printer port, Printer/Modem port, or Modem port.

- If the printer has a USB cable, plug one end into the printer. Plug the other end into a USB port on the computer or into a USB hub that's connected to the computer. (USB ports are found in newer Macs, such as the iMac and the 1999-model blue-and-white Power Macintosh G3.)

For specific directions on connecting your local printer to a computer, consult the printer's installation instructions.

When you set up a local printer, you need to make sure the necessary printer driver software is installed. You can share a local printer that uses any Color StyleWriter driver, the StyleWriter 1200 driver, or the LaserWriter 300 driver. These drivers have been included with the Mac OS for many years and, of course, are packaged with the various printer models that use them.

Install a Mac Printer Driver

The following table lists printer drivers that have been included with one or more versions of the Mac OS beginning with System 7.5.3 and the printer models that each driver lets you share. You can install additional drivers for other printers.

Printer Driver	For Sharing Printer Models
Color SW 1500	Color StyleWriter 1500, StyleWriter 1200, StyleWriter II, StyleWriter (original)
Color SW 2400	Color StyleWriter 2400 and 2200
Color SW 2500	Color StyleWriter 2500, 2400, and 2200
Color SW Pro	Color StyleWriter Pro
LaserWriter 300/LS	Personal LaserWriter LS, Personal LaserWriter 300, LaserWriter Select 300
StyleWriter 1200	StyleWriter 1200, StyleWriter II, StyleWriter (original)
StyleWriter II	StyleWriter II, StyleWriter (original)

To verify whether a printer driver is installed:

Look for the Driver

1. Open the Chooser (choose it from the Apple menu).

2. On the left side of the Chooser, you'll see icons for the printer drivers that are currently installed on the Mac. If you don't see an icon for a driver that works with your printer model, you'll need to install the appropriate driver software.

3. Close the Chooser.

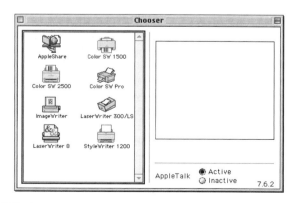

Every printer icon in the Chooser represents a printer driver file in the Extensions folder inside the System folder. Some drivers also have configuration files in the Printer Descriptions folder within the Extensions folder.

Install the Driver

To install a printer driver:

1. Open the CD-ROM or floppy disk that was packaged with your printer. Look for an **installer program** in the CD or disk content window.

2. If you see an installer program, double-click its icon and follow the displayed instructions. (Although some printer drivers can be installed without using an installer program, it's better to use one if it exists. That way, you're sure not to miss any important files or data.) At the end of the installation process, the installer will probably have you restart the Mac.

3. If the disk includes no installer program, locate the icon of the driver file in the CD or disk window and drag it to the System folder icon in the Mac hard disk content window. The Mac copies the file to the Extensions folder inside its System folder.

You can also install any of the printer drivers listed in the previous table by doing a custom installation of the Mac OS. For more information, see your Mac OS help files.

Share the Printer

To enable others on the network to share a local printer connected to a Mac, you'll make some changes in the Chooser on that Mac. You'll have the opportunity to name the shared printer, assign it a password, and establish a log of printer usage.

To set up a local printer for sharing:

1. Open the Chooser (from the Apple menu). On the left side of the Chooser, you'll see icons for the printer drivers that come with Mac OS along with icons for drivers that you have added.

2. Click to select the icon of a driver for the local printer you're going to share. If you're not sure which icon to select, review the table in the preceding section. (For instance, you can choose Color SW 2500 for a Color StyleWriter model 2500, 2400, or 2200.)

3. On the right side of the Chooser, select the port that the local printer is plugged into. If printer names are listed here as well, you can ignore them; these are the names of printers shared by other Macs on your network.

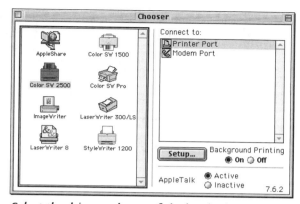

Select the driver and port of the local printer you want to share with others.

4. Click the Setup button to open the Sharing Setup dialog box for the selected printer. If you don't see the Setup button, either you selected the wrong icon on the left side of the Chooser or the printer driver doesn't support sharing.

5. Select the option Share this Printer. If this option is not present, you either selected the wrong icon on the left side of the Chooser or the printer driver doesn't support sharing.

6. Enter a name for the printer. This name will appear in the Chooser on other network Macs.

7. If you want, you can specify a password that users must enter before printing from the shared printer. Leave the password field blank if you don't want to use one.

8. If you want the Mac to keep track of who prints to the shared printer, turn on the option Keep Log of Printer Usage.

9. Click OK when you're done.

Set up sharing of a local printer; a password is optional.

After you enable sharing of a local printer, the Chooser identifies it by the name you gave it rather than by the port to which it's connected.

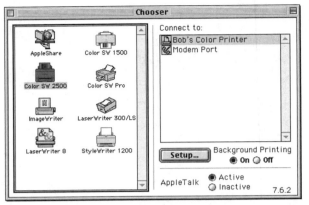

The Chooser lists a shared printer's name (not its port).

Setting Up Independent Network Printers

Independent network printers are easier to set up than shared local printers, because independent printers are inherently shared devices. You simply plug the printer into your network, perhaps assign it an IP address, and then it's available to all the computers on your network. You don't have to configure a computer to act as a host for an independent network printer.

Connect the Printer to the Network

Network printers have an Ethernet port, a serial port for a LocalTalk connector, or both. These ports are just like the ones you'll find on your computers, so you can plug a printer into your network by following the procedures described in Chapter 2 for connecting computers to the network. Here's a recap:

- **For Ethernet:** Run an Ethernet patch cable from the printer's Ethernet port to your Ethernet hub or to a nearby Ethernet wall jack.
- **For LocalTalk:** Plug a LocalTalk connector into the printer's serial port, and use a phone cord to attach the printer to your LocalTalk daisy chain network.

Using an Internal or External Adapter

If the printer doesn't have a built-in network port, you'll have to install and configure the internal or external network adapter, or print server, that was described earlier in this chapter. Installing an internal print server usually means inserting an adapter card into the printer's expansion slot. Installing an external print server usually involves connecting a cable from the printer to the print server and plugging the print server into a power outlet. After installing the internal or external print server hardware, you may have to install some software on each computer that's going to use the printer. Follow the detailed instructions included with the print server.

In some printers, including some HP LaserJet models, you can replace a LocalTalk adapter card with an Ethernet adapter card. However, you can't add Ethernet to Apple LaserWriter models that don't already have it.

Still, there are other ways to connect a LocalTalk printer to Ethernet. One method is to use an external, self-contained LocalTalk-to-Ethernet converter box such as Farallon's iPrint LT. You connect the converter to your printer's LocalTalk connector with a phone cord, and you connect the converter to your Ethernet hub or to a nearby 10BaseT wall jack with an Ethernet patch cable. The iPrint LT lets you connect not just one LocalTalk printer but a daisy-chain of up to eight LocalTalk devices to one port on your Ethernet hub.

Another solution is Apple's free utility software, LaserWriter Bridge, which you install on a Macintosh that has both LocalTalk and Ethernet connections. LaserWriter Bridge is included with some of Apple's LocalTalk printers, and it is available from Apple's Software Updates library on the Web at *http://www.info.apple.com/swupdates.*

> A Macintosh running LaserWriter Bridge must be turned on for computers connected to the Ethernet network to access the LocalTalk printer.

Here's how to set up LaserWriter Bridge:

1. Using LocalTalk connectors and cables (as described in Chapter 2), connect the LocalTalk printer to a Macintosh on the Ethernet network.

2. Install LaserWriter Bridge software on this Mac by dragging the software's icon from the installation disk to the Mac's System Folder icon (*not* to the System Folder window).

3. A message asks you to approve copying LaserWriter Bridge to the Control Panels folder. Click OK.

4. Open LaserWriter Bridge from the Control Panels folder on your hard disk. (*Don't* open the LaserWriter Bridge on the installation disk.)

5. Click the On button in LaserWriter Bridge.

6. Restart the Macintosh to make the connected LocalTalk printer available to other computers on the Ethernet network.

Connect a LocalTalk Printer to an Ethernet Network

Using LocalTalk-to-Ethernet Hardware

Using LaserWriter Bridge Software

Set Up LaserWriter Bridge

Set a Network Printer's Address

An independent network printer that uses the TCP/IP protocol must have its own IP address. The method of assigning an IP address to a printer varies from printer to printer and even among printers of the same make. You'll need to follow the instructions that came with your printer. Here we'll give you a general idea of how some printers handle IP addressing.

The rules for assigning IP addresses to computers are discussed in Chapters 3 and 4. The same rules apply to printers.

Usually, you set the printer's IP address using software running on a PC or Macintosh. Some printers require that you use a special utility program included with the printer. With other printers, you use a general-purpose Internet program, such as a Web browser.

- In some cases, you must first plug the printer into the computer's parallel port or serial port. Then you run the printer utility on the computer to set the printer's IP address. Finally, you unplug the printer from the computer and plug it into your Ethernet network.

- In other cases, the printer has a preset IP address, such as 0.0.0.0, so you can connect the printer to your Ethernet network right away. You have to change this IP address to be consistent with the other IP addresses on your network, but you can do this from any computer on the network, and you don't have to plug this printer into a computer to set the address.

Some printers can be set to get an IP address automatically from a server, such as a DHCP server, if your network has one. (Chapter 5 describes one way to add a DHCP server to your network.) With these printers, you can still manually assign a static IP address.

- Some printers that support TCP/IP will let you view the IP address on the printer's LCD display via the control buttons on the printer. Learning how to do this is a little like learning how to program your VCR; it's not always straightforward, so you'll need to follow the instructions in your printer's manual.

After setting up one or more shared printers on your network, you and other network users can print to them. All the shared printers that are available to Windows PCs on a network—including local printers shared by PCs and independent network printers that PCs can use—appear in the Network Neighborhood window of each PC. The Network Neighborhood shows you which printers are connected to your network, but your PC can't use a shared printer unless its icon appears in your PC's Printers folder.

If your Printers folder already contains an icon for a shared printer that you want to use, you're all set. You can begin printing to this printer whenever you like. If you need to add an icon for a shared local printer or an independent network printer, you can do so from the Network Neighborhood or from the Printers folder. If you're not sure whether you need to add an icon for a shared printer, go ahead and add it. Having more than one icon for a printer in the Printers folder is okay.

The quickest way to add a shared printer's icon to the Printers folder is from the Network Neighborhood. Follow these steps:

1. Open the Network Neighborhood (by double-clicking its icon on the desktop).

2. Look for the icon of the printer whose icon you want to add to the Printers folder. If the printer is attached to one of the computers on your network, you'll have to double-click that computer's icon in the Network Neighborhood to see its shared printer.

3. Right-click the icon of the printer you want to add, and choose Install from the shortcut menu. The Add Printer Wizard starts.

4. When the Add Printer Wizard asks whether anyone prints from MS-DOS programs on this PC, answer appropriately, and then click the Next button.

> If you need help on printing in general, open the Windows Help system (click Start and then click Help), click the Contents tab, and look under Print in the How To section.

Using Shared Printers from a PC

If you're using a Macintosh, not a PC, skip ahead to "Using Shared Printers from a Macintosh."

Install from the Network Neighborhood

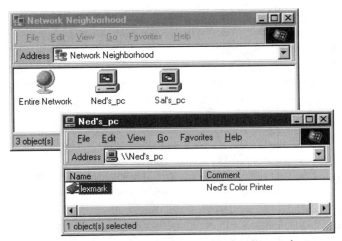

The Network Neighborhood shows network printers that you can add to the Printers folder.

5. The Wizard may now display lists of printer makes and models. Select the network printer's manufacturer in the left-hand list and the printer model in the right-hand list.

If the printer isn't listed, you'll need to provide a disk that has the printer's driver software:

- Click the Have Disk button, and in the dialog box that appears, specify the location of the driver for the network printer. Then click OK to return to the Add Printer Wizard.

- If Windows asks for the disk you specified, insert it so that the driver software can be copied to the PC's hard disk.

The printer make and model lists in step 5 don't appear if you specified a shared local printer that is **online** (meaning this PC can communicate with the printer's host PC). In this case, the Wizard will copy the driver files from the printer's host PC.

6. If the Printers folder already contains another printer's icon, and the Add Printer Wizard will ask whether you want the printer you're adding to be the default printer in Windows applications. Click Yes or No. (The default printer should be the printer you use most of the time. You can change the default printer at any time.)

7. If the printer has been assigned a password, you must enter it before you can use the printer.

8. Name the printer when you're asked. This name will appear below the printer's icon in the Printers folder on your computer. The name will appear on your computer only, not on other computers.

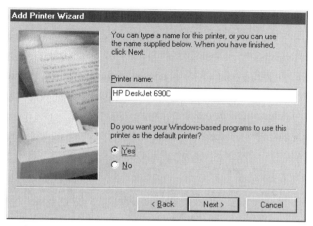

Make a network printer the default printer if you will usually want Windows applications to print to this printer.

9. The Wizard asks if you want to print a test page. Click Yes, since this is usually a good idea, and then click Next.

10. Click Finish, and Windows copies files for the shared printer to the PC's hard disk.

A new icon for the shared printer now appears in the Printers folder. The icon has a network cable at the bottom to indicate that it's a shared printer. The default printer has a check mark on its icon.

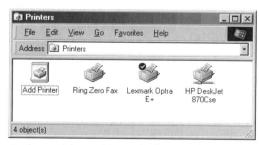

An icon with a cable at the bottom is a network printer, and the icon with a check mark is the default printer.

Change the Default Printer: To make a different printer the default printer, right-click its icon and choose Set As Default from the shortcut menu. The "Default" check mark will now appear on the selected printer's icon.

Install from the
Printers Folder

Instead of going through the Network Neighborhood to add a printer icon to the Printers folder, you can create the printer icon from **within the Printers folder** itself. This takes a little more work in the beginning because you have to specify the location of the shared printer, but the last part of both procedures is the same. Follow these steps:

1. Open the Printers folder in My Computer. Or, from the Start menu, select Settings and then Printers.

2. Double-click the Add Printer icon to launch the Add Printer Wizard, and then click the Next button to get started.

3. Select Network Printer and click the Next button.

   Network Printer means a shared printer connected to another computer or an independent printer directly connected to your network.

4. The Wizard asks you to specify the network path. (A network path looks something like this: *computer name**share name*.)

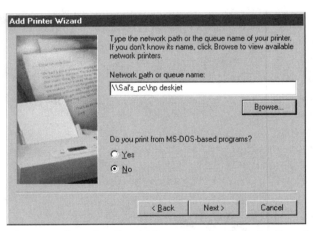

The network path tells Windows where to find the shared printer you want to use.

Browse for the
Printer's Location

5. If you don't know the printer's network path, click the Browse button. You'll see a list of the computers and independent printers on your network.

   - You can click a particular printer's icon to specify its network path. Or, to find a printer connected to another computer, double-click the computer icons in this list until you find the printer you want. Then select the printer icon.

- Click the OK button, and the network path for the printer you selected will appear in the Add Printer Wizard.

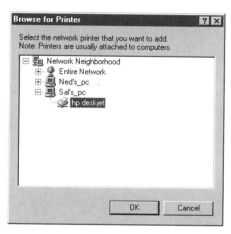

If you don't know the network path, you can look for it in this Browser dialog box.

6. The Wizard also asks you to indicate whether you or anyone on your network prints from MS-DOS applications. Answer Yes or No, and then click the Next button.

7. With the network path entered, click the OK button.

8. If the Wizard tells you the printer you specified is offline, check the network path displayed at the top of the Wizard to make sure you typed it correctly. If the path is wrong or you're not sure, click the Back button and repeat steps 4 through 6. If you're sure the path is correct, click the Next button to proceed.

*The network printer will be **offline** if the computer it's plugged into is turned off.*

9. From here, the procedure is the same as for creating a printer icon from the Network Neighborhood. Continue at step 5 of the earlier section, "Install from the Network Neighborhood."

Windows 95 and 98 don't include built-in support for the AppleTalk protocol, which some network printers use to communicate over Ethernet and LocalTalk networks. Many printers that use AppleTalk can also use other network protocols, including TCP/IP, but some printers can use only AppleTalk. These AppleTalk-only printers are designed primarily for Macintosh networks, because all Macs support AppleTalk. If you want to use an AppleTalk-only printer in a network that includes PCs as well as Macs, you can add AppleTalk capability to Windows 95 or 98 by purchasing and installing additional software.

Connecting PCs to AppleTalk Printers

Use PC MACLAN

One way to add the AppleTalk protocol to Windows is by installing Miramar Systems's **PC MACLAN** (*http://www.miramarsys.com*). Installing PC MACLAN on a PC makes AppleTalk printers appear in the PC's Network Neighborhood along with printers shared by other PCs. (PC MACLAN also lets Macs and PCs share files, as described in Chapter 7.)

As is true for any other printer, the PC with PC MACLAN must have appropriate driver software to use an AppleTalk printer. This is no problem for printers that use PostScript, and most AppleTalk printers do. Windows includes driver software for a number of PostScript printers, and additional driver software is available for Windows from printer manufacturers.

PC MACLAN does not enable printing to non-PostScript printers, such as a local StyleWriter that is shared by the Mac it's connected to. That's because Windows-based driver for these printers is not available.

As usual, you'll create an icon in the Printers folder.

To use an AppleTalk PostScript printer on a PC with PC MACLAN, you need only create an icon for it in the PC's Printers folder using the Add Printer Wizard (as described in "Install from the Network Neighborhood" and "Install from the Printers Folder").

If the Wizard asks you to select the printer make and model but doesn't list the correct combination, and you don't have a disk with Windows driver software for the AppleTalk PostScript printer, try selecting Apple in the list of manufacturers and LaserWriter II in the list of Printers. This driver may not provide access to all the features of the AppleTalk PostScript printer, but it may at least enable the PC to print on this printer.

Use DAVE

Another product, Thursby Systems's **DAVE** (*http://www.thursby.com*), takes a different approach to letting PCs use an AppleTalk PostScript printer. Installing this software on a Macintosh allows PCs on the network to access one AppleTalk printer that uses PostScript. The PCs see the AppleTalk network printer in the Network Neighborhood as a share of the Mac that's running DAVE.

To use an AppleTalk printer shared by a Mac with DAVE, you just add the shared AppleTalk printer's icon to the PC's Printers folder using the Add Printer Wizard, as described earlier in this chapter. If you can't find the Windows driver software for your particular AppleTalk PostScript printer, selecting the Apple LaserWriter II driver listed in the Add Printer Wizard may at least enable the PC to print.

Many AppleTalk printers have a parallel port as well as an Ethernet or LocalTalk port. You can plug one of these printers into a PC's parallel port, making it a local PC printer, and set up that PC to share the printer with other PCs. The local printer doesn't need to use AppleTalk or any other network protocol to communicate via its parallel port. You can keep the printer connected to your network so that Macs can still use it. The printer accepts print requests from PCs via its parallel port and from Macs via its network port.

If you have experience printing from a Mac, you'll find that accessing a shared printer via AppleTalk is similar to accessing a local printer. You indicate which printer you want to use, and it becomes the **default printer** (the active printer) to which all Mac applications print.

You can designate the default printer in the Chooser. Follow these steps:

1. Open the Chooser (from the Apple menu). On the left side of the Chooser, you'll see an icon for every printer driver installed on the Mac.

> Some icons in the Chooser have nothing to do with printing. The **AppleShare** icon, for example, is used for connecting to shared files on other Macs (as described in Chapter 8).

2. Look at the bottom right corner of the Chooser and make sure AppleTalk is set to Active.

3. Choose the icon of a driver for the shared printer that you want to designate as the default printer. The Mac OS includes printer driver software for almost all printers made by Apple Computer, as itemized in the table earlier in the section, "Setting Up a Local Mac Printer for Sharing."

> Some PostScript printers use the **AdobePS** driver or an older **PSPrinter** driver, or a PostScript driver based on one of these. Many if not all of these printers will also work with Apple's LaserWriter 8 driver.

> If you need **to install additional driver software** for a printer not made by Apple, follow the procedure described earlier in this chapter under "Install a Mac Printer Driver."

Using Shared Printers from a Macintosh

Select a Printer Driver

For more information on printing on the Mac, consult the Mac OS on-screen help. It's available from the Help menu (the question-mark menu prior to Mac OS 8) when the Finder is the active application.

More About Selecting Drivers

Attention StyleWriter and LaserWriter 300/LS Users:
To print on a shared local printer that uses any of the
StyleWriter drivers or the LaserWriter 300/LS driver, the Mac
that's going to print must have exactly the same driver version
as the Mac with the shared local printer. You can check the
driver version by selecting the icon of the printer driver in
the Extensions folder and then choosing the Get Info command
from the File menu. If necessary, copy the newest driver onto
a floppy disk and use it to replace older drivers on other Macs.

Select a
Specific Printer

4. After selecting a printer driver on the left side of the Chooser,
you select a specific printer on the right side of the Chooser. For
independent network printers, you'll see a list of printer names.
Shared local printers are listed by name along with the Mac's
printer and modem ports.

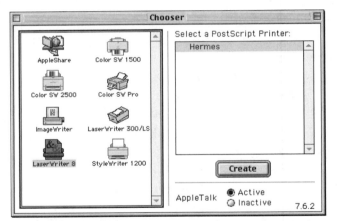

Click the LaserWriter 8 icon to see the names of PostScript
printers available on the network.

Set Up a
PostScript Printer

5. If you select a LaserWriter 8 printer in the Chooser, a Create button
or a Setup button appears below the list of PostScript printer names.
Do one of the following:

- If the **Create** button appears, click the button to begin an
automatic setup process. If you don't go through the setup
process, the LaserWriter 8 driver uses generic settings based
on the page size and features of the original LaserWriter printer.

- If the **Setup** button appears, you can click it to change the
printer's setup.

6. If you select a shared local printer (not an independent network printer) in the Chooser, a Get Info button appears below the list of ports and printer names. You can click this button to see the name of the selected printer's Mac connection, thus confirming that you have selected the printer you had in mind.

You'll also see a list of fonts that are installed on the Mac you're using but that are not present on the printer's Mac. (If you print a document containing fonts that are not present on the printer's Mac, it may print slowly or incorrectly.)

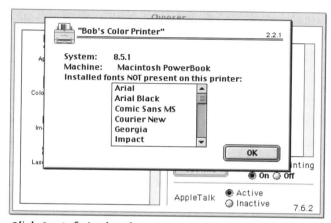

Click Get Info in the Chooser to see the name and other facts about a shared local printer's Mac.

7. When you finish selecting a driver, selecting a specific printer, and doing any necessary printer setup, you should close the Chooser. The printer you selected is now the default printer and will be used by Page Setup and Print commands in all Mac applications.

For some printers, an icon appears on the desktop after you select the printer in the Chooser. This **desktop printer icon** normally appears for printers that use any of the drivers included with the Mac OS (but usually not for printers that use other drivers). A heavy black border around the icon indicates the default printer.

You can use desktop printer icons to change the default printer and take care of other printing chores. You can also change the default printer with the Control Strip, if the Control Strip is available on your Mac.

Get Local Printer Info

Close the Chooser

Desktop Printer Icon

Bob's Color Printer

Hermes

**Connecting
Macs to Shared
PC Printers**

If your network includes PCs as well as Macs, it's not normally possible for the Macs to use a shared local printer that's connected to a PC. This is partly because Windows 95 and 98 do not normally use the same network protocol used by the Mac OS for printing . Furthermore, Macs don't include driver software for printers that connect to PCs (with the exception of PostScript printers). You can overcome these obstacles by installing additional software on your Macs.

Use DAVE

Thursby Systems's **DAVE** software enables a Mac to use PostScript printers and files shared by PCs on the same network. DAVE is a bit complicated to set up, and we don't recommend it as a solution for just printing. But if you installed it for file sharing with PCs (as described in Chapter 7), then it'll also let your Macs use PostScript printers that are otherwise available only to the PCs on your network.

DAVE implements Microsoft networking software protocols on a Macintosh. With DAVE installed, PostScript printers connected to and shared by PCs will appear in the Chooser when you select the LaserWriter 8 icon. However, DAVE does not enable Macs to print to non-PostScript printers shared by PCs. It doesn't supply any printer drivers.

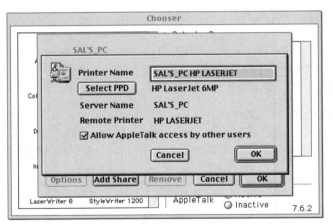

DAVE software enables Macs to use PostScript printers shared by PCs.

Another option is to install Miramar Systems's **PC MACLAN** on the PC. The PC MACLAN Print Server program lets Macs use the same printers used by PCs on the network, provided the Macs have appropriate driver software.

Sal's PC LaserJet

PostScript printers made available this way can use the LaserWriter 8 driver. These printers simply show up in the Chooser when you select the LaserWriter 8 icon. But PC MACLAN by itself doesn't enable printing to non-PostScript printers shared by PCs. For that, you need to install additional driver software on the Mac. (PC MACLAN also lets Macs and PC share files, as described in Chapter 7.)

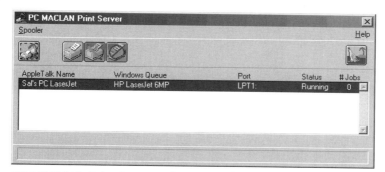

PC MACLAN's Print Server makes PostScript printers connected to PCs available on Macs.

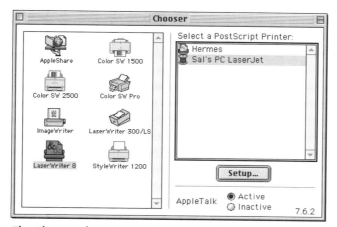

The Chooser shows PostScript printers that are connected to PCs and shared by PC MACLAN.

Non-PostScript PC Printers

Ordinarily, a Mac can't print to shared printers connected to PCs if they don't use the PostScript printer language. A Macintosh simply doesn't have the drivers needed to use these printers.

You can, however, add printer drivers with a product called PowerPrint Networks from InfoWave (*http://www.infowave.com*). It supplies a Mac with printer drivers for more than 1600 printers that use the PCL printer language and other non-PostScript printer languages.

Summary

The desire to share a printer among several computers is reason enough to install a network. A network gives everyone access to a top-notch printer yet costs less than equipping every computer with a mediocre printer.

▼ You can share **local printers** that are connected directly to computers and independent **network printers** that are connected directly to your network.

▼ To share a printer, you'll need a physical connection for it as well as software for the network connection and the **printer driver** software.

▼ **To share a local printer with other PCs**, you need to plug the printer into the PC's parallel port or USB port; install the driver software on the PC; install the Windows network software for file and printer sharing; set parameters for Windows control of access to your shared printer; and designate the local printer as a shared printer.

▼ **To share a local printer with other Macs**, you need to plug the printer into a Mac serial port; install the driver software on the Mac; and designate the local printer as a shared printer.

▼ **Network printers** are easier to set up than local printers, because they're inherently shared devices. You simply plug the printer into your network and perhaps assign it an IP address. Then it's available to the computers on your network.

▼ Before a PC can use a shared local printer or a network printer that appears in its Network Neighborhood, the **printer icon must appear in the PC's Printers folder**. You can add a shared printer from the Printers folder or the Network Neighborhood in Windows 95 or 98. You can also enable PCs to use AppleTalk printers by installing additional software.

▼ To use a **shared printer on a Mac**, you use the Chooser to designate the shared printer as the default printer. (The Mac must have the compatible printer driver in its Extensions folder.) You can install software that enables Macs to use some printers shared by PCs.

Share Files with Others

7

A network makes floppy disks all but obsolete. No longer must you walk floppies or Zip disks from one computer to another to share your files. Instead you can set up **file sharing** on your network—which lets you copy, open, and save files on other computers as easily as you can on your own hard disk. Don't worry; setting up file sharing doesn't necessarily mean that it's open season on your files and everyone using your network has access to them. You can restrict access to your data in several ways. For example, you can allow access only to specific folders on your computer rather than to your entire hard disk, or you can require that a password be entered to gain access to your computer's hard disk.

Although the procedure for sharing files is somewhat different between a Windows PC and a Macintosh, you can share files across platforms. This chapter explains how to make files on one computer available to the other computers on your network. The other half of file sharing—accessing those shared files from another computer—is covered in Chapter 8.

Sharing Files with Other Windows PCs

Both Windows 95 and 98 include all the software a PC needs to share files with other Windows PCs on your network. Using this software involves completing the following tasks:

- Make sure the network software for file sharing is installed on the computer.
- Set the parameters for how Windows will control access to all the computer's shared folders and disks.
- Designate those folders or disks whose contents you want to share.
- Set access restrictions for each shared folder or disk.
- Monitor file-sharing activity.

The first four of these tasks must be done on each PC whose files you want to make available on your network; the last task is optional. None of these tasks is necessary for a PC that will *not* make its own files available but will use shared files of *other* computers.

Before you set up file sharing, make sure the network adapter, protocol, and client software are installed and configured, as described in Chapter 3.

Installing the File Sharing Service

The **Windows file-sharing software** may already be installed on the PC. For instance, a PC that's set up to share its local printer (as described in Chapter 6) already has the necessary software installed. It's also possible that the file sharing software was installed when Windows was installed. In either case, you need to make sure file sharing is configured correctly. Use the **Network dialog box** to see if the PC has been properly set up with file sharing software.

The Windows software that allows a PC to share its local printer also allows the PC to share its files.

To install Microsoft File and Print Services:

1. Open the Control Panel and double-click the Network icon. The Network dialog appears with the Configuration tab on top.

2. Look for "File and printer sharing for Microsoft Networks" in the list of installed network components. If you find this network component listed, skip ahead to the section "Setting Access Control." If you don't see this network component listed, you need to install the network component that provides the file sharing service.

Look for
this line

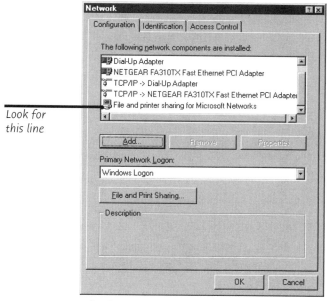

Check to see whether file and printer sharing software is already installed.

3. Click Add to open the Select Network Component Type dialog box.

4. Choose Service as the type of network component you want to install, and then click Add.

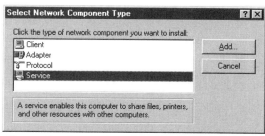

Choose Service as the type of network component to add.

5. In the next dialog box, you'll select the File and Printer Sharing software, as follows:

- **Windows 98 users** see a dialog box listing several services. Select "File and printer sharing for Microsoft Networks" and click OK.

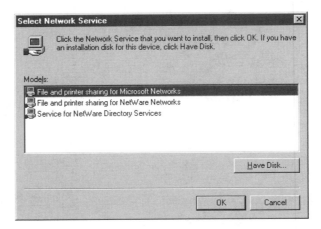

- **Windows 95 users** see a dialog box with two lists. In the Manufacturers list, select Microsoft; then select "File and printer sharing for Microsoft Networks" in the Network Services list. Click OK.

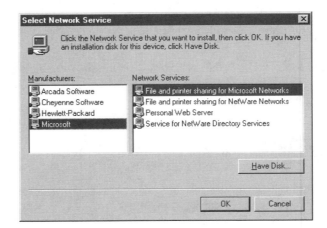

6. Windows may now ask you to insert your installation CD-ROM so it can copy the file sharing software to your hard disk. Go ahead and follow the prompt.

7. Scroll the list at the top of the Configuration tab of the Network dialog box. You should see "File and printer sharing for Microsoft Networks" listed.

8. Click the button labeled File and Print Sharing.

9. In the File and Print Sharing dialog box, select the option "I want to be able to give others access to my files." (For file sharing, it doesn't matter whether the other check box is selected or not.) Click OK to return to the Network dialog box.

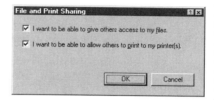

The next step in making your PC's files available for sharing is to determine how Windows controls access to the shared folders. On a peer-to-peer network, you can control access only by assigning passwords to each shared folder and disk, as described shortly. This is called **share-level access control**.

Setting Access Control

To set the access control method:

1. In the Network dialog box, click the Access Control tab to open it.

2. Select the option for share-level access control.

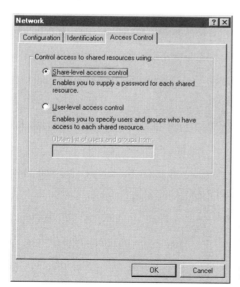

Share-level access control is the only method available on a network without a Windows NT server.

3. Click the OK button to close the Network dialog box.

Windows may ask you to insert the Windows CD so that some files can be copied to your hard disk. After copying, Windows will ask you to restart your computer. You can do that now, or press on.

The other method of controlling access to shared items (**user-level access control**) is not available unless your network has a Windows NT server. Server-based networks are not covered in this book. If you add a Windows NT server to your network, you can select user-level control in the Access Control tab of the Network dialog box. In this case, each person who uses the network has an individual password, and you can specify which users or groups of users have access to each shared folder and disk.

Selecting Folders to Share

Windows uses the term "share" to describe any directory (that is, any folder or disk) that you allow other computers to access over your network. The process of making a folder or disk a share is called **creating a share**. (The same term applies to shared printers, as described in Chapter 6.)

Before making a folder a shared item, think carefully about its name and location. If you move or rename the folder, or any folder or disk in its path, the shared item will no longer be shared. Avoid changing a folder's path after making the folder a shared item.

To share a folder or disk:

1. Locate the icon of the folder or disk you want to share, either in Windows Explorer or by clicking My Computer and finding it there.

2. Right-click the icon to open its shortcut menu. Then select Sharing.

3. Click the Shared As option on the Sharing tab in the Properties dialog box.

4. In the Share Name field, type in a name for the folder or disk. This name

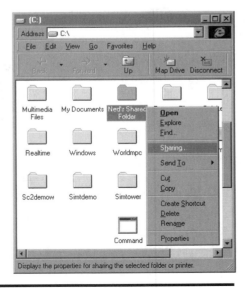

will appear in the Network Neighborhood of all PCs on your network. You can use the same name as the folder or disk itself, or you can call it something different. The name can have no more than 12 characters.

> When naming a folder or disk, you can hide the item from the Network Neighborhood of other (unauthorized) users by appending a dollar sign ($) to the name. This gives you greater control over who can use the shared item, because anyone who wants to access it will have to know its exact name and will need to map a drive letter to it (see Chapter 8 for more about this).

5. In the Comment field, type a phrase that describes the shared item or its location. If this PC has more than one shared folder or disk, the comment will help users identify this one.

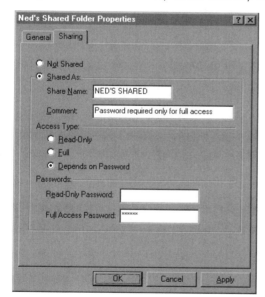

The Share Name and Comment can be seen by other network users; passwords are optional.

Changing the name of a share on your computer can make it more difficult for others to use. That's because networked PCs will still display the old share name in the drop-down Path list of the Map Network Drive dialog box, because they don't know that you changed the name (as described in Chapter 8.) If someone tries to select the old name from the share list, they'll get the error message "Share name not found." To use the renamed shared item, they'll have to learn the new name and type it in.

Restrict Access to Files

6. Choose an option to restrict access to the share. The bottom half of the Sharing tab in the Properties dialog box contains options for **restricting access**. Under the heading Access Type, you'll see three choices that restrict access: Read-Only, Full, or Depends on Password.

> **Cable Modem Users:** *Always* specify passwords if you use a cable modem connection to the Internet. If you leave a password field blank, any neighbors with PCs and cable modems will be able to access your shared folders on their PCs.

- **Read-Only**: Users on other network PCs will be able to see and open the files in a Read-Only shared folder or disk, but they won't be able to make changes to the files or copy new files into the shared folder or disk. Nor will they be able to delete files from the shared folder or disk. They will be able to copy files from the shared folder or disk to their own hard disks.

- **Full**: This option allows people using other network PCs to read and write to files on this shared folder or disk. In other words, network users can see and open, copy, save changes to, and delete files on this folder or disk.

- **Depends on Password**: This access type lets you set two different passwords for connecting to the shared folder or disk—one password is for Read-Only access, and the other grants Full access. Each password can be no more than eight characters in length.

To allow Read-Only access without a password and Full access with a password, set the access type to Full, leave the Read-Only Password blank, and then enter a password for the Full access Password.

Look for the Hand Icon

7. Click OK to finish making the folder or disk a shared item. Take a look at the shared item's icon, and you'll see that it now sports a hand image to indicate the item is shared. The folders and disks you designate as shared items will appear in the Network Neighborhood of the PCs on the network. (Chapter 8 explains how to connect to shared folders and disks over the network.)

You can see who is currently connected to a PC's shared items by opening the **Net Watcher utility**. This utility is normally buried several levels deep in the Start menu (point to Programs, then Accessories, System Tools, and then Net Watcher).

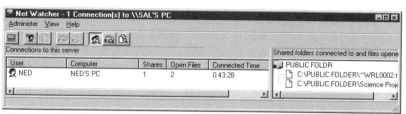

Oversee shared items with Net Watcher.

Net Watcher shows you what shared items are available on the PC, who is currently connected to them, and which files are open on other network computers. You can change your view of the network activity by clicking one of the buttons in the toolbar or by selecting an equivalent command in Net Watcher's View menu.

Other toolbar buttons and menu items allow you to take action on connected users, shared folders, and open files. As detailed in the following paragraphs, these controls allow you to disconnect individual network users, close a file that someone has open, stop sharing any shared item, share additional items, and change access restrictions, right from your computer.

Click the **Show Users button** to list the users who are currently accessing this PC's shared items. From this list, you can select a user to see which shared items the user is conneceted to.

Show/Disconnect Users

To disconnect a user, select the user in the list and then click the **Disconnect User** button on the toolbar.

Click the **Show Shared Folders button** to see a list of all the shared items that are available on this PC. From the list, you can select a shared item to see whether anyone is connected to it.

Show Shared Folders

You can perform several operations on the shared folders listed here. To stop sharing an item, select it and click the **Stop Sharing button** on the toolbar. To change access restrictions from this list, select the item you want to change and then select **Shared Folder Properties** from the Administer menu. To make another shared item, click the **Add Share button** on the toolbar and specify the path of the item you want to share.

Show Files

Click the **Show Files button** to list this PC's files (from its shared folders) that are now open on another network computer. You can close a file by selecting it in the list and then clicking the **Close File button** on the toolbar.

Sharing Files with Other Macs

A Macintosh includes all the software it needs to share files with other Macs on your network. **File sharing software** is a standard part of the Mac OS (since System 7, circa 1991), so you won't need to install anything unless you have a really old Mac. Of course, you do need to set up the file sharing software. On each Mac whose files you want to share, you need to perform the following simple tasks:

- Turn on file sharing.
- Designate the folders and disks whose contents you want to let others share.
- Set access privileges for each shared folder and disk.
- Set the Guest access for the whole computer.

These tasks are necessary only for Macs whose files will be shared. None of these tasks is necessary on a Mac that will not share its own files but will use shared files from other computers. Let's take a look at these Mac file-sharing tasks.

You don't need to restart a Mac after you change its file sharing setup. This includes turning file sharing on and off, making a folder or disk shared or not shared, and changing a shared item's access privileges.

Turn File Sharing On/Off

Until file sharing is turned on, a Mac can't share its files with other computers on the network. To turn on file sharing, go to the File Sharing control panel of Mac OS 8 or later, or the Sharing Setup control panel of Mac OS 7.6.1 or earlier.

To turn on Mac OS file sharing:

1. Open the File Sharing control panel. Click the Start/Stop tab (Mac OS 8 or later), or open the Sharing Setup control panel (Mac OS 7.6.1 or earlier). Make sure the Owner Name, Owner Password, and Computer Name fields are filled in (as described in Chapter 4).

2. Click the upper Start button (the one under "File Sharing Off" or "File Sharing"). The button changes to a Cancel button while file sharing starts up, which may take a little while. When file sharing is on, the button becomes a Stop button.

Other Shared Services:

Turning file sharing on or off has no effect on other network services, such as sharing an Internet connection or playing games.

Program Linking: You can ignore the Program Linking section at the bottom of the control panel. It has no effect on file sharing.

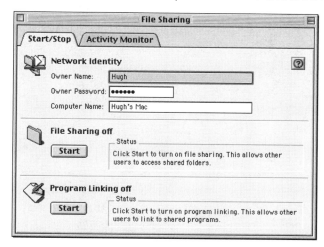

The File Sharing control panel in Mac OS 8 and later.

The Sharing Setup control panel in Mac OS 7.6.1 and earlier.

When you turn off your Mac's file sharing capability, you prevent other computers from using its shared items, but your computer can still use shared items on other computers.

To turn off file sharing, click the Stop button in the File Sharing or Sharing Setup control panel. A dialog box appears, in which you set a number of minutes until file sharing is turned off. During this interval, your computer notifies other networked computers about the change. Users on computers that are connected to your computer's shared items are notified of how long they have until the "file server" shuts down. You can set the delay period to zero to stop file sharing immediately, but users on other computers will be disconnected without warning.

Turning Off File Sharing

You can set a polite interval before file sharing turns off.

If your Mac has a **Control Strip**, you can use it to turn file sharing on and off. Just click the File Sharing button, which looks like a folder icon, and choose the appropriate command from the pop-up menu.

The File Sharing button in the Control Strip.

Selecting Folders to Share

Once Mac file sharing is turned on, you can designate shared items. You can share folders and disks, including hard disks, CD-ROMs, Zip disks, and most other removable disks that appear on the Mac's desktop. However, you can't share floppy disks or the folders on them.

You can designate up to 10 folders and disks as shared items. Folders nested inside a shared item do not count toward this limit. Network users can connect to the shared items via the Chooser or Network Browser, as described in Chapter 8.

Nested Folders: You cannot make a folder a shared item if it is nested within a folder that is already a shared item. Network users can access the inner folder by connecting to the outer shared folder, or you can move the inner folder to the desktop or to another folder, where it can be made a separate shared item.

To share a folder or disk:

1. Select the folder or disk icon in the Finder.

2. Display the sharing info for the selected folder or disk:

- **Mac OS 8.5 and later**: From the File menu, choose Get Info and then Sharing.

- **Mac OS 8.1 and earlier**: From the File menu, choose Sharing.

In Mac OS 8 and later, you can use a **contextual menu** to display the sharing info for a folder or disk. Simply Control-click the folder or disk icon to pop up its contextual menu. Then choose Sharing from the Get Info submenu (Mac OS 8.5 and later) or choose Sharing directly from the contextual menu (Mac OS 8–8.1).

3. Select the option "Share this item and its contents."

4. If you want to lock the shared folder, select the option "Can't move, delete, or rename this item." A locked folder can't be moved to another folder, be dragged to the Trash, or have its name changed by anyone. Enabling this option does not, however, prevent anyone from dragging files and folders into or out of the shared folder.

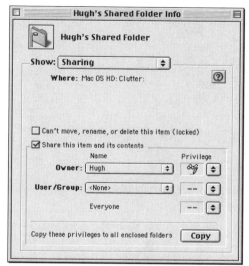

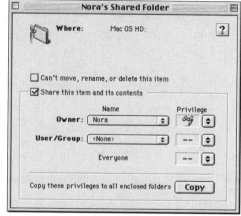

A folder's sharing info in Mac OS 8-8.1.

A folder's sharing info in Mac OS 8.5 and later.

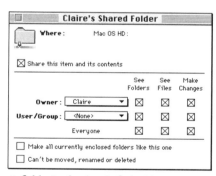

A folder's sharing info in Mac OS 7.6.1 and earlier.

You can lock *any* folder by turning on the option "Can't move, delete, or rename this item" in its sharing info. The folder does not have to be shared (the option "Share this item and its contents" does not have to be selected) to be locked.

Setting Basic Access Privileges

To limit what network users can do with the contents of a shared folder or disk, you can set **access privileges**. You have a great deal of flexibility in setting access privileges, as described in the upcoming section "The Ins and Outs of Access Privileges." But if you'd rather keep it simple and avoid the details, you can set privileges according to one of the following basic scenarios:

Basic Privileges for Minimum Security: This arrangement gives all network users full access to the shared item's contents:

- In Mac OS 8 and later, set Everyone to Read & Write.
- In Mac OS 7.6.1 and earlier, turn on all the Everyone privileges, including See Folders, See Files, and Make Changes.

Basic Privileges for Maximum Security: In this arrangement, you require network users to know a Mac's owner name and password to use the contents of a shared folder or disk.

- In Mac OS 8 and later, set Everyone to None, User/Group to None, and Owner to Read & Write.
- In Mac OS 7.6.1 and earlier, turn on all of the Owner privileges and turn off all the User/Group and Everyone privileges.

If you use the maximum security setup described here, you can make it easier for network users to use shared items by entering the same owner name and password in the File Sharing or Sharing Setup control panel on all Macs in the network. (Each Mac still must have a unique computer name, however.) Having a common owner name and password isn't as secure as having different names and passwords, but it's a lot less stuff to remember.

Once you've shared a folder, its icon sprouts a network wire to let you know it is shared. In addition, faces appear on a shared folder's icon when someone is connected to it from another Mac. The icon for a disk, however, does not change when you make it a shared item.

Setting Guest Access

In addition to setting access privileges for each shared folder and disk, you need to determine whether to allow guests to connect at all. **Guests** are unidentified network users who can connect without a password. In Mac OS 8 and later, by default, guests are *not* allowed to connect; but in Mac OS 7.6.1 and earlier, they are allowed to connect.

To turn Guest access on or off:

1. Open the Users & Groups control panel.

2. Double-click the Guest icon in the Users & Groups window.

3. From the Show pop-up menu in the Guest window, choose Sharing. (In Mac OS 8.1 and earlier, you won't need to do this step.)

4. If you want to allow unidentified network users to connect, turn on the option to "Allow guests to connect to this computer"; otherwise, turn it off.

5. Close the Guest window and the Users & Groups window.

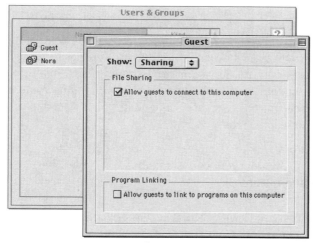

Turn Guest access on to allow any network user to use shared folders and disks without a password.

Attention Cable Modem Users: If you have a cable modem connection to the Internet, make sure Guest access is **turned off**. Remember that every Mac in your neighborhood with a cable modem is part of your local network. With Guest access turned off, your neighbors can't connect to a shared folder or disk unless they know a name and password that's listed in your Mac's Users & Groups control panel. This warning does not apply to other Internet connection methods, including regular modems, ISDN, and DSL.

Protection for Shared Files: If you'd like to simplify your life by turning on Guest access but are concerned about the security of some of your Macs, keep in mind that you can protect a Mac's data by turning off file sharing. For instance, you can enable file sharing on the Macs in your kids' rooms but disable it on your home office Mac. This lets you move files between your Mac and the shared folders on your kids' Macs, but it prevents your kids from getting into folders or disks on your Mac. And keep in mind that you don't have to have file sharing turned on all the time. You can turn file sharing on, move some files, and then turn it off.

The Fine Points of Mac File Sharing

What you've read so far about controlling access to shared items on your Macintosh barely scratches the surface of the possibilities. Many other alternatives are available to you for setting access privileges, adding users and groups, monitoring shared items, inheriting access privileges, keeping enclosed folders private, changing ownership of a folder, and getting the same users and groups on all Macs. In this section we'll explore each of these topics.

If you're happy with the simple access control alternatives described so far in this chapter, you can skip ahead to "File Sharing Between Windows and Macintosh."

Ins and Outs of Access Privileges

If you're not satisfied with setting access privileges according to one of the basic scenarios, or you simply want to know more about how privileges work, you'll need to learn about the categories of users and the privilege levels you can set for each category. Then you'll be able to get more creative in limiting what network users can and can't do with a shared item.

User Categories

As explained in the following sections, you can set explicit access privileges for three categories of users: Owner, User/Group, and Everyone.

- **Owner**: Initially, the owner of a folder or disk is the person named as the owner in the File Sharing or Sharing Setup control panel. This is usually the person who works on the Mac most of the time. If the Mac is used by several people, the owner could be the person who manages your network (probably you). If you specify the same owner name and password on all your Macs, everyone who knows the password will have owner privileges.

- **User/Group**: You can designate one network user or a group of users to get special access privileges. To utilize this category, you must register users and groups in the Users & Groups control panel, as described shortly in "Adding Users" and "Adding Groups."

- **Everyone**: The Everyone category includes users who are registered in the Users & Groups control panel and who may have passwords. This category also includes guests (unidentified users without passwords) if Guest access is enabled in the Users & Groups control panel.

You don't have to set privileges for the Owner or User/Group categories if they have the same privileges set in the Everyone category, especially if the Everyone category has full access privileges.

For each of the user categories, you can set explicit access privileges. In **Mac OS 8 and later**, you choose a privilege level from a pop-up menu. In **Mac OS 7.6.1 and earlier**, you set privileges by turning check boxes on and off in any combination. The following two tables explain the access privilege settings according to their respective Mac version.

Privilege Levels

Access Privilege Levels (Mac OS 8 and Later)

	Privilege Level	Permissions Granted
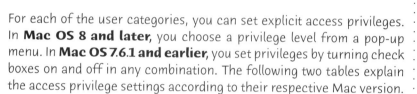	Read & Write	Users can see and open all the files and folders in the shared folder or disk and can copy files from it. Users can also save changes to files and add files.
	Read only	Uses can see and open all the files and folders in the shared folder or disk and can copy files from it. Users can't save any changes to files or copy files to the shared folder or disk.
	Write only	Users can add files to a shared folder or disk but can't open it.
	None	Users can't see, open, or add to the shared folder or disk.

Access Privilege Settings (Mac OS 7.6.1 and Earlier)

Privilege	Permissions Granted	Similar Privilege in Mac OS 8 and Later
See Folders	Users can open the shared folder or disk, can see and open folders in it, and can copy folders from it.	N/A
See Files	Users can see and open files in the shared folder or disk and can copy files from it.	N/A
Make Changes	Users can add files and folders to the shared folder or disk. Users can't open the shared item to create, delete, move, and change files or folders unless See Files or See Folders is turned on.	Write only
See Folders and See Files	Users can see and open files and folders in the shared folder or disk and can copy items from it.	Read only
See Folder, See Files, and Make Changes	Users can add files and folders to the shared folder or disk; and can create, delete, move, and change files and folders that are inside the shared folder or disk.	Read & Write

When You Upgrade... Several possible combinations of privilege settings are available in Mac OS 7.6.1 and earlier that don't exactly correspond to privilege levels in Mac OS 8 and later. However, Mac OS 8 and later will honor settings made in versions 7.6.1 and earlier, allowing your network to include Macs with older and newer versions of the Mac OS. If Mac OS 8 or later encounters a combination of privilege settings that don't correspond to one of its privilege levels, the system will display a question mark icon instead of a glasses and pencil, glasses only, or pencil only icon.

Adding/Removing Users As described earlier, you can allow everyone to access a Mac's shared folders and disks, or you can allow only the owner to have access. But you don't have to settle for only these two alternatives. You can use the **Users & Groups control panel** to identify individual network users and groups of network users, granting or denying them special access privileges to your shared items.

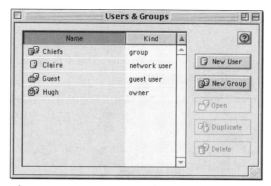

The Users & Groups control panel in Mac OS 8 and later.

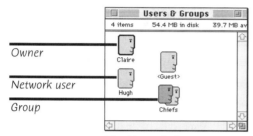

The Users & Groups control panel in Mac OS 7.6.1 and earlier.

Each user is represented in the control panel by an icon, and each user except Guest has a unique name and can have a password. The Owner name and password are taken from the File Sharing or Sharing Setup control panel. Initially, each Mac has two users in its Users & Groups control panel: the Owner and Guest. When you add new network users to the Users & Groups control panel, you assign their names and passwords as well.

> Macintosh file sharing, unlike its Windows counterpart, doesn't need a dedicated server to have **user-level access control**. Each Mac stores its own list of users who will access it.

To add a network user:

1. Open the Users & Groups control panel.

2. Click the New User button (or, in Mac OS 7.6.1 and earlier, choose New User from the File menu).

An icon named New User appears in the control panel, and if you're using Mac OS 8 or later, the icon opens to display the user's window and the user name is selected for editing. If you're using an earlier version, the icon does not open but the user name is selected for editing below the icon.

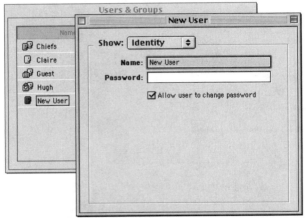

Adding a new Macintosh file sharing user in Mac OS 8 and later.

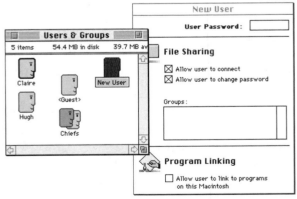

Adding a new user in Mac OS 7.6.1 and earlier.

3. Type a name for the new user. You can use any name, but it's most convenient to use the same name that this person has entered in the Owner Name field of his or her own File Sharing or Sharing Setup control panel. This is the name that will be supplied automatically when the user tries to connect to another Mac, as described in Chapter 8.

> For simplicity and clarity, make sure each registered user has the same name on all network Macs. Don't use "Elizabeth" on one Mac, "Liz" on another, and "Beth" on a third, for example.

4. If the user's window is not already displayed, open the user's icon. Type a password in the user's window; use a different password for each person. You can leave the password blank if you don't want to require the user to enter one.

5. If you want, turn on the option to "Allow user to change password"; the user will be able to replace the password with one that's easy for him or her to remember.

6. Close the user's window.

> User names and passwords are meant to identify individuals, not computers. If several people share the same computer, add a separate user item in the Users & Groups control panel for each person. But keep in mind that a user name and password are not positive proof of identity. Anyone who learns someone else's user name and password can access your shared folders and disks as an impostor.

To remove a network user:

▼ Drag the user's icon to the Trash.

or

▼ Select one or more user icons and click the Delete button or choose Delete from the File menu. (The Delete button does not exist in Mac OS 7.6.1 and earlier.) Users are deleted immediately. They don't wait in the Trash until you empty it, as do many other deleted items.

Adding Groups

With Macintosh file sharing, you can add groups of network users and give the group special access privileges for a shared folder. For instance, you could give a group full access to a folder to which everyone else has partial access.

To add a group:

1. Open the Users & Groups control panel.

2. Click the New Group button (or, in Mac OS 7.6.1 and earlier, choose New Group from the File menu).

   An icon named New Group appears in the control panel, and if you're using Mac OS 8 or later, the icon opens to display the group's window with the group name selected for editing. If you're using an earlier version, the icon does not open but the group's name is selected for editing below the icon.

3. Name the group.

Adding Users to a Group

You can add members to a group in any of these ways:

- Drag users from the Users & Groups window into the group window.

- Drag users to the group icon in the Users & Groups window.

- In Mac OS 8 and later, drag one group to another group, in which case all the members of the dragged group become members of the other group.

   You can select several users (as you would select multiple icons in the Finder) and drag them together to a group icon or window.

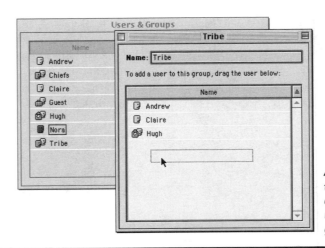

Add members to a group by dragging their icons to the group window.

To remove a user from a group, drag the user's icon from the group window to the Trash. If you're using Mac OS 8 or later, you can also remove users by selecting their icons in the group window and pressing the delete key, or by choosing Remove from the File menu.

Removing users from a group

Once you set up file sharing, it hums along in the background. Network users connect to your Mac's shared folders without your knowledge. If you're ever wondering who is connected, or you want to review which folders and disks are shared items, you can use the Activity Monitor tab of the File Sharing control panel (if you use Mac OS 8 or later). In Mac OS 7.6.1 and earlier, a separate control panel called File Sharing Monitor provides the same information.

Monitoring File-Sharing Activity

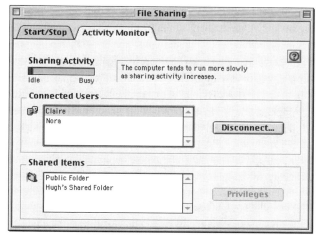

In Mac OS 8 and later, File Sharing's Activity Monitor tab shows which items are shared and who is connected.

In Mac OS 7.6.1 and earlier, the File Sharing Monitor shows which items are shared and who is connected.

Disconnecting Users

You can disconnect any user by selecting the user's name in the control panel's list of connected users and then clicking the Disconnect button. A dialog box asks how many minutes' delay you want to allow before the user is disconnected, and the user will be notified in advance of the approaching disconnection. You can enter 0 minutes to disconnect a user without warning.

Changing Privileges or Share Status

With Mac OS 8 and later, File Sharing's Activity Monitor tab makes it easy to change access privileges for, or even stop sharing, any shared item. Simply double-click the item in the list of shared items, or select the item and click the Privileges button, to display the item's sharing info (shown earlier in "Selecting Folders to Share"). There you can set different access privileges or stop sharing the item by turning off the option "Share this item and its contents." Close the sharing info window to make any changes take effect.

Inherited Access Privileges

Initially, all folders enclosed in a shared folder or disk inherit their access privileges from the shared folder or disk. If you change the privileges of the shared folder or disk, the privileges of the enclosed folders also change. Move an enclosed folder to a different shared folder, and the enclosed folder inherits the privileges of its new enclosing folder.

Setting Independent Privileges

You can explicitly set privileges for any enclosed folder, independent of the shared folder that encloses it, as follows:

1. Click to select the enclosed folder in the Finder.
2. Use the Sharing command to bring up the selected folder's sharing info. (**Mac OS 8.5 and later**: From the File menu, choose Get Info and then Sharing. **Mac OS 8.1 and earlier**: Choose Sharing from the File menu.)
3. Turn off the option "Use enclosing folder's privileges" (Mac OS 8 and later) or the equivalent option "Same as enclosing folder" (Mac OS 7.6.1 and earlier).
4. Set the privileges you want for the enclosed folder.
5. Close the sharing info window.

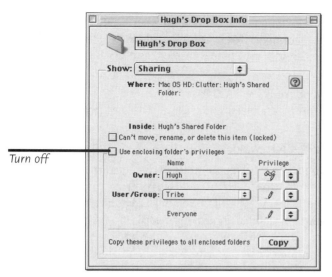

Turn off

Setting independent privileges for a folder enclosed in a shared item (Mac OS 8 and later).

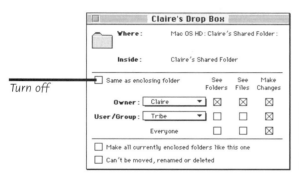

Turn off

Setting independent privileges for a folder enclosed in a shared item (Mac OS 7.6.1 and earlier).

After you have set independent privileges for an enclosed folder, it retains them even if you move it to a different enclosing folder. To make an enclosed folder inherit the privileges of its enclosing folder, turn on "Use enclosing folder's privileges" or "Same as enclosing folder" (depending on the Mac OS version).

You can force folders to use the same privileges as the folder or disk that encloses them by taking these steps:

1. Select the folder or disk that has the privileges you want to force on its enclosed folders.

Forcing Inherited Privileges

2. Use the Sharing command to display the sharing info for the enclosing folder or disk. (**Mac OS 8.5 and later**: From the File menu, choose Get Info and then Sharing. **Mac OS 8.1 and earlier**: From the File menu, choose Sharing.)

3. Click the Copy button (Mac OS 8 and later) or turn on the option "Make all currently enclosed folders like this one" (Mac OS 7.6.1 and earlier).

4. Close the sharing info window.

When you force a folder to inherit privileges, this action coincidentally stops all affected folders from *automatically* inheriting any subsequent changes you might make to the privileges of the enclosing folder or disk. If you change the enclosing item's privileges, none of the enclosed folders is updated automatically. To propagate the change to the enclosed folders, you have to explicitly repeat the steps just above for forcing inherited privileges.

File Sharing Between Windows and Macintosh

What we've covered so far about file sharing on Macintosh computers and Windows PCs won't help you set up file sharing between Macs and PCs on the same network. For that, you need more than the software and commands included with Windows and the Mac OS. You have three alternatives:

- Use Internet technology, such as a simple Web server.
- Add specific cross-platform file sharing software to the PCs or the Macs.
- Add a dedicated file server that can handle both platforms.

Let's take a closer look at each alternative.

Web Technology for Cross-Platform Sharing

Included with **Mac OS 8 and later** is a feature called **Personal Web Sharing** that can be used to share one folder or one disk with any other computer that has a Web browser. Obviously, this includes PCs with Windows. Personal Web Sharing creates a personal Web site on your network, and this site can list the contents of one Mac folder or disk. Network users can connect their Web browsers to this site to gain access to the contents of the folder or disk, including the contents of enclosed folders.

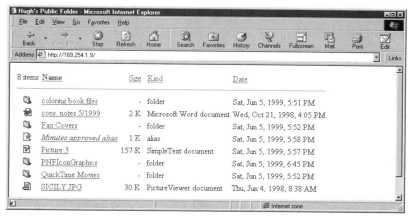

A Windows Web browser can access folders and files on a Macintosh that has the Personal Web Sharing utility. Notice that the Windows user sees file icons as they appear on the Mac.

Network users who access files through Personal Web Sharing will be able to open only certain types of files, including text files, within their Web browsers. For other types of files, such as Microsoft Word files, users will have to copy the files to their computers and then open the copies. In contrast, all other forms of file sharing allow users to open the original files directly.

Setting Up Personal Web Sharing

Mac OS 8 and Later

Here's how to use Personal Web Sharing to share a folder:

1. Make sure the Mac has the TCP/IP protocol configured, as discussed in Chapter 4.

2. Turn on file sharing in the File Sharing control panel, as described earlier in this chapter.

3. Select the folder or disk you want to share. Then use the Sharing command (from the File menu, choose Get Info and then Sharing) to make it a shared item, as described earlier in this chapter.

4. Open the Web Sharing control panel.

5. Click the upper Select button, next to the words "Web Folder: ..." In the dialog box that appears, select the folder or disk you want to share.

6. Click the lower Select button, next to the words "Home Page: ..." In the dialog box that appears, click None. This setting indicates that you want Personal Web Sharing to list the contents of the folder you selected in step 5.

7. At the bottom of the control panel, select the option "Use File Sharing to control user access." This tells Personal Web Sharing to control access to the folder or disk you selected in step 5 by using the access privileges you set up with ordinary Mac file sharing.

8. Click the Start button.

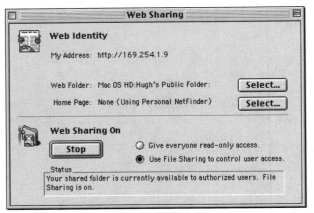

Set up the Web Sharing control panel to list the contents of one folder or file on your personal Web site.

Your Web Site's Address

After Web Sharing has started up, the address of your personal Web site appears at the top of the Web Sharing control panel in the My Address line. On most small networks, this address will contain a numeric IP address such as http://169.254.1.9, not a Web-site name such as http://www.peachpit.com. Tell network users your address so they can point their Web browsers to it and see the shared folder or disk and its contents.

Security Issues

User Name and Password: When network users try to connect to your personal Web site, they may be asked to enter a user name and password. This is the name and password you have set up in your Users & Groups control panel, as explained earlier in this chapter. Network users do not have to go through this authentication process, however, if you select the option "Give everyone read-only access" in the Web Sharing control panel.

Enter Network Password

Please enter your authentication information.

OK

Cancel

Resource: Web Sharing

User name: Andrew

Password:

☐ Save this password in your password list

*Network users can be required to enter a user name
and password to see the shared folder or disk on
your personal Web site.*

**Connecting to the Internet with Web Sharing turned
on opens the possibility of someone on the Internet
accessing your shared folder or disk**. If all the Macs on
your network share an Internet connection, it's possible that
all the Macs with Web Sharing turned on will be open to
intrusion by someone else on the Internet when any one of
your networked Macs makes an Internet connection. However,
if your Internet gateway has a firewall feature (as described
in Chapter 5), you should be protected. If you're not sure
about the firewall, you can prevent Internet invaders from
accessing your Macs' personal Web sites by turning on the
option "Use File Sharing to control user access" in the Web
Sharing control panel. Then turn off Guest access in the
Users & Groups control panel on each Mac.

Software for Cross-Platform Sharing

The Personal Web Sharing solution to cross-platform file sharing is not
as convenient as regular file sharing, and it doesn't let PC users share
their files with Macintosh users. To enable your Macs to participate
fully in Windows file sharing, like PCs, you can add some specific cross-
platform file sharing software. Alternatively, you can add software to
the PCs, enabling them to participate fully in Mac OS file sharing. Your
choice will likely be based on whether you have more Macs than PCs,
or vice versa. With either solution, the Macs and the Windows machines
will be able to access each other's files.

DAVE

Thursby Software's DAVE makes a Mac capable of using Windows file
sharing. A Mac with DAVE installed can connect to folders and disks
shared by PCs on the network. Conversely, the Mac can create
Windows-style shares that show up in the Network Neighborhood of

the PCs. Because you must buy DAVE for each Mac that needs cross-platform file sharing, this solution is a good way to add a couple of Macs to a mostly Windows network. For more information, contact Thursby Software at *http://www.thursby.com*.

PC MACLAN

Printer Sharing:

DAVE and PC MACLAN also work for cross-platform sharing of printers. See Chapter 6.

Miramar Systems' PC MACLAN makes a Windows PC capable of using Macintosh file sharing. With PC MACLAN installed, a PC can connect to folders and disks shared by Macs on the network. In addition, the PC can designate Mac-style shared items that appear in the Chooser and Network Browser of the Macs. If you have fewer PCs than Macs, you'll buy and install less software by getting PC MACLAN for each PC that needs cross-platform file sharing. (You can contact Miramar Systems at *http://www.miramarsystems.com*.)

Adding a Dedicated File Server

The third way to enable file sharing between Windows and Macintosh machines is to add a **file server** that serves both platforms. This solution is expensive, however, because you must buy the server software and install it on a dedicated server computer. No one works directly on the dedicated file server computer—it only stores and serves files for other computers on the network. The file server computer can be a PC or a Mac.

The most popular server software that runs on a PC is **Microsoft's Windows NT Server**. It includes software called Services for Macintosh, which you install separately from Windows NT itself. Services for Macintosh enables Macintosh users to access the same files as Windows users. If you don't have any experience or training with Windows NT, Services for Macintosh can be a bit complex, and you might want to consider hiring a consultant to set it up for you.

If you want a Macintosh-based server, **AppleShare IP 6.0** (and later) serves files to both Windows and Macintosh computers. This is a standard feature; you don't have to install any separate software to support Windows users. AppleShare IP is also the easiest server to set up. Where Windows NT Services for Macintosh treats Mac users separately, Windows and Mac users are served together in AppleShare IP. Anyone capable of setting up file sharing on a Macintosh should be able to set up AppleShare IP without assistance.

We've barely mentioned the use of dedicated servers in this book. That was intentional. You don't need to buy an expensive dedicated server and software to operate a small network with PCs or Macs or both. Because of the expense and added complications associated with the use of dedicated servers, and because they're not necessary (although they are powerful), servers aren't covered in this book.

You may think you don't need to bother with network security inside your own home or office. But are you sure you want your kids' friends or all your coworkers to have access to every shared file on your computer? There are various strategies for securing your shared files, some of which we've mentioned earlier in the chapter. Let's review.

Security Reminders

- First, you don't need to turn on file sharing on every computer to move files back and forth. If you enable file sharing on your kids' computers (for instance) but not on your home office computer, you'll be able to move files back and forth from your computer, but the kids won't be able to accidentally open your investment portfolio (or other personal data) from their computers.

- You've seen that adding passwords on Windows machines and Macs isn't all that difficult. But you don't have to password-protect everything. If you want to share some files without a password, consider creating a special public folder and putting these files in it.

- You can choose to share individual folders rather than your entire hard disk.

- On a Mac, consider turning off the Owner's permission to see all disks that aren't shared items. This leaves fewer files at risk in the event someone learns your owner name and password. You set this permission by opening the owner icon in the Users & Groups control panel.

- If you have a cable modem connection to the Internet, you are at particular risk from your neighbors who also have cable modem connections. That's because all the cable modems in a neighborhood of several hundred cable TV customers are interconnected in one big local network. If your home network connects to the Internet via cable modem, be sure that all your computers with file sharing turned on require passwords, and make sure these passwords remain secure.

Summary

File sharing eliminates the need to tote files from one computer to another on a floppy or Zip disk. Both Windows and the Mac OS let you designate folders and disks as shared items whose contents other people can access from other computers on your network. You then set access controls that determine who can read and write files on your computer. Windows and Mac OS have different procedures for setting up file sharing.

▼ In **Windows**, you must first **install the service** "File and printer sharing for Microsoft Networks" in the Network dialog box.

▼ You **control access in Windows** by assigning passwords to each shared folder or disk. Each folder and disk can have one password for Read-Only access and another password for Full access.

▼ You use the **Net Watcher utility** to see who's connected to a PC's shared folders and disks.

▼ On a **Macintosh**, the **file sharing software** is pre-installed, but you can turn it on or off.

▼ You control access on a **Mac OS** by setting **access privileges** for each shared folder and disk. You can set access privileges separately for three categories of network user: Owner, User/Group, and Everyone. You can set each category's privileges to Read & Write, Read only, Write only, or None.

▼ If you don't want to allow unidentified Mac users to connect without passwords, you can turn off all **Guest access**.

▼ To identify Mac network users and groups of users, you add them to the **Users & Groups** control panel.

▼ In Mac OS 8 and later, the **Activity Monitor** tab of the File Sharing control panel lists connected users and shared items. The same information appears in the **File Sharing Monitor** control panel in Mac OS 7.6.1 and earlier.

▼ Folders can **inherit access privileges** from the folder that encloses them, or each enclosed folder can have its own access privilege settings.

▼ **To share Mac files with Windows PC users,** you can use the Personal Web Sharing feature of Mac OS 8 and later. **To enable a PC to use Macintosh file sharing,** install Miramar Systems' PC MACLAN on the PC. To give a Mac the ability to use Windows file sharing, install Thursby Software's DAVE on that Mac.

▼ For the ultimate in cross-platform file sharing, hang a dedicated file server on your network. Windows NT Server is the most popular server software for PCs, as is AppleShare IP for Macs. Both serve files to Windows and Macintosh machines.

▼ File sharing makes your computers more **vulnerable to invasion,** especially if your network shares a cable modem connection to the Internet. You can take several steps to secure your shared files.

Use Other Computers' Shared Files

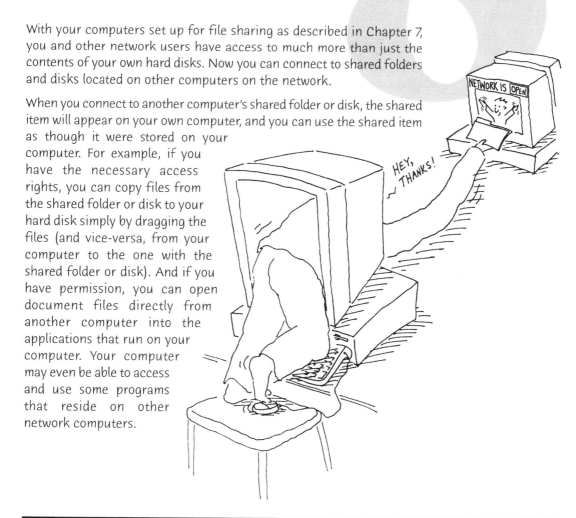

With your computers set up for file sharing as described in Chapter 7, you and other network users have access to much more than just the contents of your own hard disks. Now you can connect to shared folders and disks located on other computers on the network.

When you connect to another computer's shared folder or disk, the shared item will appear on your own computer, and you can use the shared item as though it were stored on your computer. For example, if you have the necessary access rights, you can copy files from the shared folder or disk to your hard disk simply by dragging the files (and vice-versa, from your computer to the one with the shared folder or disk). And if you have permission, you can open document files directly from another computer into the applications that run on your computer. Your computer may even be able to access and use some programs that reside on other network computers.

Browsing Your Network

Mac Users: *On a Macintosh, the owner of the shared folder may limit your ability to see its contents, as discussed later in this chapter.*

Both Windows and Mac OS have tools for **browsing** your network to find shared folders and disks. Windows has the **Network Neighborhood**, and Mac OS has the **Chooser** and the **Network Browser.** All of these tools show you the network computers with shared folders or disks that are currently available, and from there you can connect to them. Once you're connected, you can view the shared item's files and folders using Windows Explorer or the Macintosh Finder.

Using Other PCs' Shared Files

All the shared folders and disks available to Windows PCs on your network appear in the Network Neighborhood of each PC. The Network Neighborhood icon is located on the Windows desktop and in the Windows Explorer. When you click on either icon, you'll see a window with icons of the PCs on the network that have file sharing enabled.

Your Own Workgroup

Network
Neighborhood

The PCs you first see in the Network Neighborhood are those in the same workgroup as your computer. (You named your workgroup in Chapter 3, using the Identification tab of the Network dialog box.) If you don't see the computers on your network displayed, double-click the Entire Network icon to find them.

Multiple Workgroups

On bigger networks, the Entire Network window will display computers that are part of other workgroups. Depending on the arrangement of your network, you may see icons representing other workgroups or one or more **domains.** (A domain is a group of computers associated with a Windows NT Server, which is beyond the scope of this book.) To access the computers that belong to another workgroup or domain, double-click the workgroup or domain's icon.

Changing the View:

As for other windows, you can use the View menu to change the view of the Network Neighborhood between large icons, small icons, and a list.

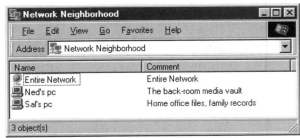

Inside the Network Neighborhood.

You can connect only to folders shared by computers that are currently turned on. The Network Neighborhood doesn't display icons for computers that are turned off.

The Network Neighborhood displays computers that use any of several network protocols, the most common on small networks being TCP/IP and NetBEUI. It's most efficient if every PC on your network uses the same protocol for file sharing and if unused protocols are removed from all the computers' Network dialog boxes. Of course, it may be necessary to keep multiple network protocols for purposes other than file sharing, such as multiplayer gaming. For instructions on adding and removing protocols, review Chapter 3.

A Word About Protocols

Does Your Network Have Macs? With Windows 95 and 98, the Network Neighborhood does not display computers that use the AppleTalk protocol, which is the standard for Macintosh file sharing. If your network includes Macs, you can make them appear in the PC's Network Neighborhood by installing cross-platform file sharing software such as DAVE or PC MACLAN, which are described in Chapter 7.

You can connect and use the shared folders and disks around your network in several ways:

Connecting to Shared Items

- Via the Network Neighborhood
- By using shortcuts on the desktop
- By using a mapped drive letter

To connect to a shared folder or disk on another computer:

1. In the Network Neighborhood on your PC, double-click the network computer that stores the shared folder or disk that you want to access.

Connect from the Network Neighborhood

You'll see an itemized display of that computer's shared folders and disks, as shown on the next page. (You'll also see the network computer's shared printer, if it has one.)

2. Double-click the shared item that you want to use.

3. If the shared item has been assigned a password, you'll need to enter that password in the dialog box that appears.

All shared disks look like folders in the Network Neighborhood.

Shared items can require two passwords; entering one password grants you read-only access to the shared item, and entering the other password grants you full access.

183

4. The shared item opens, showing you the folders and files it contains. The shared item's window looks and acts just like the windows that you see on your own computer.

If the person who set up the shared folder or disk assigned it read-only access, you won't be able to save files in that folder or copy files to it.

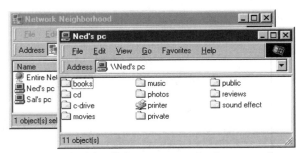

When you double-click a computer in the Network Neighborhood, you see its shared folders and disks.

Connect Using a Windows Shortcut

A quick way connect to a shared folder or disk is via a shortcut that you add to your desktop. You create the shortcut in the usual manner:

- Hold down the right mouse button, and drag the shared folder or disk from the Network Neighborhood to the desktop. Release the mouse button to open the shortcut menu, and then select Create Shortcut(s) Here.

The shortcut icon will appear on the desktop. Now you can connect to the shared folder or disk and open it at the same time by double-clicking the desktop shortcut.

Use Mapped Drive Letters

Another way to connect to a shared folder or disk is to **map a drive letter** to it. Just as your floppy drive is designated by the letter A:, and the hard drive is (usually) designated by C: (unless you changed it), you can assign an unused drive letter, such as E:, to a shared folder or to a disk from another computer. The result is a **network drive**, which appears in all the places on your computer that typically display your computer's own local drives (such as My Computer and Windows Explorer).

To map a shared folder to a drive letter:

1. In the Network Neighborhood, right-click the shared folder or disk that you want to map.

2. From the menu that appears, choose Map Network Drive.

3. A dialog box called Connect Network Drive appears, displaying the next available drive letter. You can keep this letter or choose another letter if you wish. You'll see the path to the shared folder or disk displayed below the Drive field.

4. If you want to connect to the shared folder or disk automatically every time you start Windows, select the "Reconnect at logon" option.

5. Click the OK button.

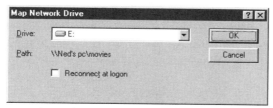

Mapping a drive letter to a shared folder or disk.

When you map a shared folder to a drive letter, the shared folder looks and acts just like a drive attached to your PC. You'll be able to access it from the same places where you can normally open a file on your computer. This includes the Open and Save dialog boxes of software applications, the My Computer window, and Windows Explorer.

Using Your Network Drives

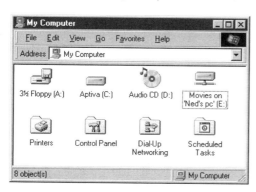

A shared folder mapped to a drive letter appears in the My Computer window.

You can even access a file on the shared folder from a command line, like this: *e:/movies/1984.mov*

Use the command line, too.

Specifying the Path: Another method for mapping a network drive is especially handy for shared folders and disks you have used before.

- From the Tools menu of any Windows Explorer window, choose Map Network Drive. (This command is also on the shortcut menus that pop up when you right-click the My Computer or Network Neighborhood icon.)

- You'll see a variation of the Map Network Drive dialog box, where you can specify the path of the shared folder or disk that you want to map to a drive letter. Typing a long path is no fun, but you can click the arrow at the end of the Path field to select a path from a drop-down list of paths you've previously accessed.

Disconnecting a Mapped Drive

After mapping a network drive, you may later decide to disconnect it. Simply right-click the Network Neighborhood or My Computer icon to open the shortcut menu; then select Disconnect Network Drive. A dialog box appears listing the drive mappings currently in effect, where you can select the drive you want and click OK to disconnect it. (This same Disconnect Drive command also appears in the Tools menu of Windows Explorer.)

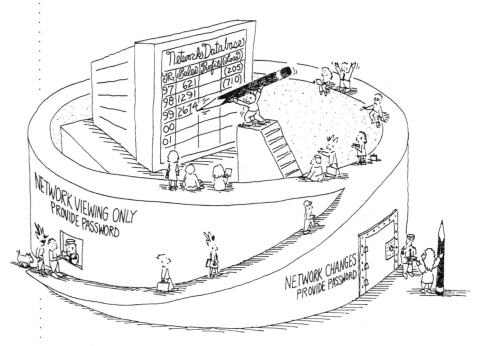

You may find that you've been disconnected from a shared folder or disk or that it no longer appears in the Network Neighborhood as a shared item. As discussed in Chapter 7, the availability of shared items is controlled by the person using the computer that stores those items.

Where's That Folder?

If your network includes Macs, each Mac can connect to the other Macs' shared folders or disks in several ways:

- Via the Chooser
- Via the network Browser (in Mac OS 8.5 or later)
- By using an alias of a shared item

Using Other Macs' Shared Files

The traditional network browser for Mac OS has been the Chooser. For over a decade, it has been the place to see which computers have shared folders and disks available on a network. It also acts as a place to select network printers, as discussed in Chapter 6. Amazingly, the Chooser has hardly changed at all since the days of the first Macs.

Connecting from the Chooser

To use the Chooser to connect to shared items:

1. Open the Chooser from the Apple menu at the top-left corner of the screen. You'll see icons on the left portion of the Chooser and a blank area on the right. Most of the icons in the Chooser represent printer drivers, but the **AppleShare icon,** used for file sharing, is also located there.

2. In the bottom-right corner of the Chooser, make sure the AppleTalk option is set to Active.

What are file servers?

On a small Mac network, **file servers** are simply Macs with file serving turned on. If your network includes a PC on which PC MACLAN cross-platform file sharing is installed (as described in Chapter 7) then PC MACLAN is also listed as a file server.

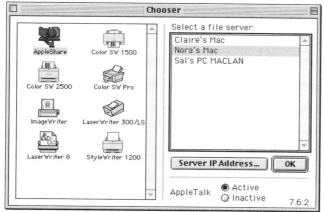

Select the AppleShare icon in the Chooser to see a list of Macs with shared folders and disks.

3. Click the AppleShare icon on the left. A list of file servers appears on the right.

> **Chooser Protocols**: The Chooser lists Macs that use the AppleTalk protocol—the protocol that Macs normally use for file sharing. If your small network has a dedicated AppleShare file server that uses the AppleTalk protocol, the Chooser will list that server as well. If file servers that use the TCP/IP protocol have been added to your network, these servers will not be shown in the Chooser. You can still connect to them, however, by clicking the **Server IP Address** button and typing the server's IP address (for example, 169.254.1.9), which you can get from the file server's owner.

4. To see the folders and disks shared by one of the computers listed on the right side of the Chooser, double-click the computer's name.

Establish Your Identity

5. A dialog box asks you to establish your identity. You may be able to connect as either a registered user or a guest.

- If you select **Registered User**, you must enter the name and password that you have been assigned *for the computer you're connecting to.* You don't have to enter the name if it's the same as the Owner name from your File Sharing or Sharing Setup control panel, because the system automatically fills this in for you. Type the password carefully and correctly, including capitalization (it's case-sensitive).

- If the **Guest** option is available (not dimmed), you can select it to connect without entering a name or password. A guest usually has restricted access to shared folders and disks, so it's usually better to connect as a Registered User if you can.

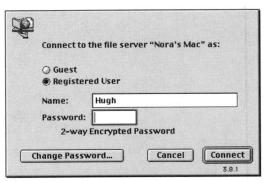

Establish your identity as a Registered User or a Guest

Owner's Special Privileges: If you're connecting to your own computer from another one, enter the owner name and password specified *on your computer*. As owner, you may have full access to the computer's disks whether they have been designated as shared items or not. This is handy if you need access to your computer's files while you're away from your computer. (The owner's special access can also be turned off, as explained in Chapter 7.)

6. While connecting as a registered user, you may be able to change your password. Click the Set Password button, and a series of dialog boxes will lead you through the process of changing your password.

   If you get a message saying your password couldn't be changed, you probably don't have permission to change it. This permission is set in the Users & Groups control panel on the computer you're connecting to, as described in Chapter 7.

7. When you click OK after establishing your identity, another dialog box lists the shared items available on the computer you're connecting to. You can select one or more of these shared items. To select more than one item, Shift-click each one.

   If a listed item is dimmed, either you are already using it or the owner of the item hasn't given you permission to use it.

8. If you want, you can specify that you want a folder or disk to **connect automatically** every time you start up the Macintosh. To do this, select the checkbox next to that item. If you select a checkbox and are connecting as a Registered User (not as a Guest), two options appear below the list of items.

   - **Save My Name Only** indicates that you want your Mac to ask you for the password when it starts up, before it connects to the specified folders or disks. Use this option to prevent people from restarting your computer to gain unauthorized access to shared folders or disks.

   - **Save My Name and Password** indicates that you want your Mac to supply your password automatically when it opens the checked item during startup.

Optionally Change Your Password

Selecting Shared Items

Safety Feature

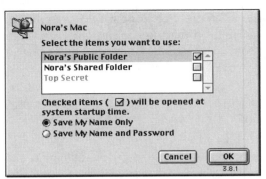

Select shared folders and disks to which you
want to connect.

Nora's Public Folder

A Network Disk Icon

9. After you click the OK button, a **network disk icon** (also known as a network volume) appears on the desktop for each of the shared items that you selected. Mac OS considers any shared folder or shared disk to be a kind of disk; you use a network disk like one of your own computer's disks.

Connecting with the Network Browser

The Network Browser, an alternative to the Chooser, is included with Mac OS 8.5 and later. The process for connecting to a shared network volume with the Network Browser is more streamlined than using the Chooser.

To use the Network Browser to connect to shared folders and disks:

1. From the Apple menu, open the Network Browser.

You'll see a list of the network Macs with file sharing turned on. Included in the list are PCs that have the PC MACLAN cross-platform file sharing software (described in Chapter 7).

If nothing appears in the Network Browser, make sure the AppleTalk control panel is set up correctly (review Chapter 4).

2. Click the disclosure triangle next to a listed computer to see its shared folders and disks.

3. A dialog box asks you to establish your identity. This is the same dialog box you encounter when you use the Chooser (see step 5 in the preceding section, "Connecting from the Chooser"). You can connect as a Registered User, in which case you must enter the name and password assigned to you *on the computer you're connecting to*. Or, if the computer allows Guest access, you can connect anonymously without using a password.

4. At this time, you may also be able to change your password (see step 6 in "Connecting from the Chooser").

5. The Network Browser lists the shared folders and disks available on the computer whose disclosure triangle you clicked. Items you are already connected to are listed. Items for which you don't have permission are not listed.

6. Double-click a shared item, and a network disk icon appears for it on the desktop. In addition, the Finder automatically opens the shared item for you.

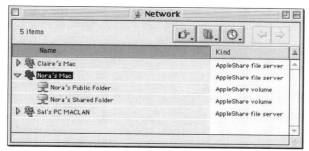

The Network Browser can list network computers and their shared items in one window.

The Recent Button: You can save time when reconnecting to a shared folder or disk that you've recently connected to. Click the Recent button (the one with the clock icon); its pop-up menu lists recently accessed items. Choose something in this menu, establish your identity as usual, and the shared item opens in the Finder.

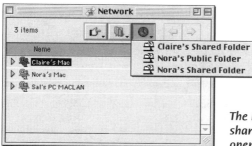

The Recent menu lists shared items you have opened recently.

Browser vs. Chooser:

The Network Browser lets you select only one shared item, and the item opens automatically after you click it. The Chooser lets you select multiple shared items from the same network computer, but they do not open automatically. The Chooser lets you designate shared items to be reconnected automatically when your computer starts up; the Network Browser doesn't do this.

Like the Chooser, the Network Browser lets you connect to an AppleShare IP server or to a computer with shared folders that uses the TCP/IP protocol instead of AppleTalk. Click the Shortcuts button (the button with the pointing finger), and from the pop-up menu choose Connect to Server. Then type the IP address of the computer to which you're connecting.

Connect with a Macintosh Alias

The **quickest way to connect** to another Mac's shared folder or disk is to use an **alias** of it or of any file or folder it contains. You can make an alias of a file, folder, or disk shared by another network computer just as you would make an alias of an item on your own computer. For example, if you're using Mac OS 8 or later, hold down the Option and Command keys while dragging the original shared item to the place where you want its alias to appear.

You can use the alias of a shared item in the same way you would use the original item. Double-click the alias to open the original; drag an item to the alias of a folder or disk to add the dragged item to the original folder or disk; and so on. The alias contains all the information necessary for connecting to the original item over a network.

When you use an alias of an item from a shared folder or disk that you're not presently connected to, the system automatically makes the connection over the network. You'll see the usual identification dialog box, in which you enter your name and password. The name that you used to connect when you made the alias will already be filled in for you (you can also enter a different name if you want). If you were connected as a Guest when you made the alias, the connection is made without the identification dialog box appearing at all.

Making Aliases in the Network Browser: You can also make an alias of a shared folder or disk directly from the Network Browser. To do this, simply drag a shared folder or shared disk from the Network Browser window to the desktop. If you drag a listed computer (not a shared disk or folder) from the Network Browser, you get a **network location file** that refers to the computer. Double-clicking this file opens the Network Browser and displays a list of the computer's shared folders and disks.

You can move any alias icon anywhere on your computer, and it will still work. In fact, you can copy the alias to a floppy disk and carry it to any other Mac on the network and the alias will work from there. Double-clicking the alias right from the floppy will allow you to connect to the original file, no matter where on the network the alias happens to be located.

Your Access Privileges

After connecting to a shared folder or disk, you may find that the owner has limited your access to its contents by setting **access privileges** as described in Chapter 7. The owner can set access privileges separately for each shared folder or disk and each folder enclosed in a shared folder or disk. You may be allowed to open a folder; you may be restricted to adding information to it; or you may be forbidden access. If you try to do something that you're not authorized to do, an alert will appear to tell you about the problem. Special folder icons also indicate your access privileges, as shown here:

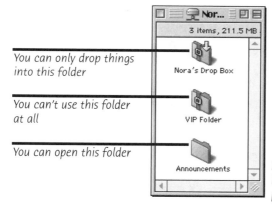

You can only drop things into this folder

You can't use this folder at all

You can open this folder

Folder icons indicate access privileges.

If you are allowed to open a folder, you may not be allowed to see files or folders in it or make changes to items inside. Your privileges are indicated by small icons located just below the folder window's close box, as shown here:

Can't see files   Can't see folders   Can't make changes

Icons in windows indicate access privileges you have been denied.

Disconnecting from Shared Items

To disconnect your Mac from another Mac's shared folder or disk, drag the shared item's desktop icon to the Trash, just as you would if you were ejecting a CD-ROM or floppy disk. Or you can select the shared item's icon and choose Put Away from the File menu.

You can also be disconnected involuntarily from a network computer by the person using it (as discussed in Chapter 7).

When you disconnect from a shared folder or disk, you also disconnect from the computer storing the shared item—unless your Mac is still connected to another shared folder or disk from the same computer. While your Mac is connected to another computer, you can connect to additional shared folders and disks without entering your user name or password again.

If you want to reconnect to a network computer using a different user name, you must first remove the icons of all its shared folders and disks from your desktop. Then you can enter a different name the next time you use the Chooser, Network Browser, or an alias to connect to the same computer.

Summary

When file sharing is set up on some of the computers in your network, you and other users can connect to the folders and disks designated as shared items.

▼ While connected to a shared folder or disk, you can use its contents as though the shared item were on your own computer.

▼ Browse your network to determine which computers have shared folders and disks available. With Windows, use the Network Neighborhood. With the Mac OS, use the Chooser or Network Browser.

▼ Before connecting to a shared folder or disk, you may have to enter a user name and password.

▼ In Windows, you can map another computer's shared folder to an unused drive letter on your computer. Then the shared folder conveniently appears as a drive, similar to any drive attached directly to your computer.

▼ For quick access to a shared item, you can create a Windows shortcut for it on your PC or a Macintosh alias for it on your Mac.

▼ On a Macintosh, folder icons and icons in window headers show your access privileges to shared folders.

▼ You can disconnect a shared item from your Macintosh by removing its icon from your desktop, and you can completely disconnect your Macintosh from another computer by removing all its shared items from your desktop.

Serious Fun and Games

9

Even if you've set up every network service we've discussed so far—sharing files, printers, and an Internet connection—you haven't begun to tap the potential of your little network. Spend some money for new software, and you can extend the functionality of your network for fun and profit. You can play computer games with other players, share an electronic calendar and address book, send messages, or back up files to a central location for safekeeping. Using the network, you can even control another computer and operate software that isn't installed on your computer.

Playing Games on Your Network

A network can add a whole new dimension to computer game playing. Instead of battling or racing a predictable (and often invincible) computer, you can match wits and skill with a real human sitting at another computer.

Many types of games can be played over a network, including shoot 'em ups, racing games, strategy games, board games (chess, for instance), and casino-type games. You can join games against opponents over the Internet, as well as those on your own local network. In this chapter, we'll focus on using your local network for **multiplayer gaming**.

Prepare Your Computers

As with other network activities such as file sharing, multiple copies of a game must communicate over your network. Games communicate using the TCP/IP or IPX/SPX **network protocol**. On a **Mac-only network**, many games communicate using the AppleTalk protocol. Some games offer a choice of network protocols; others require a particular protocol. Before playing a game on your network, find out what protocol it uses and make sure the protocol is set up on the appropriate computers.

TCP/IP Settings

These days, most games require the TCP/IP protocol. Because it's the protocol of the Internet and is commonly used for printer and file sharing in Windows 95 and 98, TCP/IP is probably already set up on your computers. If not, you'll find instructions for setting up TCP/IP in Chapters 3 (for Windows) and 4 (for Macintosh).

Attention Mac Users!

If you have a Mac with its own dial-up connection to the Internet (not a shared connection as described in Chapter 5), you need to change the **configuration** of the Mac's **TCP/IP control panel** whenever you switch from using the Internet to a local network service that also uses the TCP/IP protocol—including multiplayer games.

For local network services, the TCP/IP control panel's Connect Via option must be set to the network port to which your network is connected—usually Ethernet, Alternate Ethernet, or Ethernet Slot x (where x identifies a slot with an internal Ethernet adapter). By comparison, the Connect Via setting for a dial-up Internet connection is PPP. To easily switch configurations, set up named configurations as described in Chapter 4.

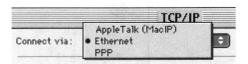

Set each Mac's TCP/IP control panel to connect via the local network port (not via PPP).

If you try to use a TCP/IP service on your local network while the control panel's Connect Via setting is at PPP, your Mac will dial up the Internet. This happens because in Mac OS 8.6 and earlier, the Open Transport networking software can use only one TCP/IP configuration at a time. This is particularly problematic with software that runs automatically at startup, such as the Retrospect backup software described later in this chapter.

Some games offer the option of using the IPX/SPX protocol, but this protocol probably isn't set up on your computers because it isn't used much for anything but games these days. Fortunately, IPX/SPX is easier to set up than TCP/IP.

Setting Up IPX/SPX in Windows

On a Windows PC, you first need to install the IPX/SPX protocol in the Network dialog box, as described in Chapter 3. Then you need to make sure the Frame Type setting is the same on all the computers.

To configure the IPX/SPX protocol in Windows 95 or 98:

1. Open the Network dialog box with the Configurations tab on top. (Click Start, Settings, and Control Panel, and then double-click the Network icon.)

2. In the list of network components, select the listing that combines IPX/SPX and the network adapter to which your local network connects.

3. Click the Properties button to display the IPX/SPX Properties dialog box.

4. Click the Advanced tab.

5. In the Property list on the left, click Frame Type, and in the Value list on the right, select Ethernet 802.3.

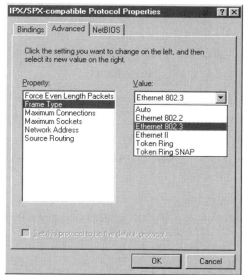

Select the IPX/SPX frame type in Windows.

Buy in Bulk

*To run the network services and activities described here, you'll have to get new software for most if not all of your computers. Fortunately, many software publishers offer discounts when you buy for several computers. Often you'll buy a **license** to install multiple copies of the software. Do the math and you can save money.*

6. In the Property list, click Maximum Connections, and make sure the Value setting is 16.

7. In the Property list, click Maximum Sockets, and make sure the Value setting is 32.

8. Click OK to accept the changes to the Properties box, and then click OK in the Network dialog box.

> **Follow the game instructions**: The settings made in the foregoing steps are the IPX/SPX settings most games use. If you are using IPX/SPX, you should read the installation instructions with your game to see if its settings differ.

Setting Up IPX in Mac OS

The IPX/SPX protocol is also available for Mac OS, and some Mac games use it. If a game uses IPX/SPX, the game will include MacIPX extension and control panel files; drag these files to the System Folder icon (*not* the System Folder window) and they will be routed automatically to the correct folders inside the System folder.

To configure the IPX/SPX protocol on a Macintosh:

1. Open the MacIPX control panel.

2. Double-click the Ethernet icon to bring up the Ethernet Access Configuration dialog box.

3. Turn off the Always Auto-Configure Frame Type option, select the Ethernet 802.3 option, and then click OK. If a message appears telling you that existing network services may not work due to the changes you made, click OK (don't worry about it).

4. Close the control panel.

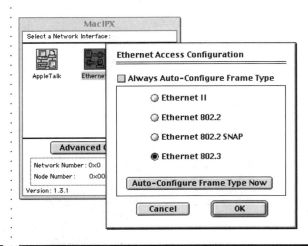

Set the IPX/SPX frame type on a Macintosh.

Follow the game's instructions: The settings made in the steps above are the IPX/SPX settings that most games use; however, you should check the installation/operation instructions that come with your game to see whether its settings differ.

Each game has a highly unique look and feel, so you won't encounter many windows or menus that are "standard" or even similar in game software. You'll also find that games adapt differently to network play. In some games you oppose other network players rather than computer-generated foes; in other games you'll join forces with other network players to achieve a common goal.

To give you a feel for some variations of network gaming, let's take a look at a few popular titles: Quake, Star Wars: X-Wing Alliance, StarCraft, and NASCAR Racing.

Quake from id Software is a classic shoot 'em up computer game with several sequels, each as popular as the original. In an ordinary Quake game you shoot grotesque monsters—an arguably noble goal. But a multiplayer Deathmatch game shaves off some of the fantasy veneer by pitting you against other players over the network—an arguably uncivilized goal. In Quake 2, each player is represented by a character on the screen, and you can tailor your character as you wish. Each character has a different name, so when your character is blasted, you know who killed it.

Try it out: You can get a free, abridged version of Quake 2 for Windows at id Software's Web site (*http://www.idsoftware.com*).

Quake 2 Deathmatch requires that each computer playing the game use the TCP/IP protocol. It also requires that you designate one of the computers to be the Network Server. This can be any player's computer, or it can be a network computer that no one is currently using. Before starting a Deathmatch game, you need to set up the Quake Network Server. Then each player can join the game from his or her own computer.

To set up a Quake Network Server:

1. Start Quake. A movie will begin. (Press the Esc key if you want to skip the movie and get to the main Quake menu.)

Examples of Network Games

Quake

Set Up a Multiplayer Quake Game

2. Use the up- and down-arrow keys to move the Quake cursor icon to the Multiplayer option in the Quake menu. Press the Enter key to go to the Multiplayer menu.

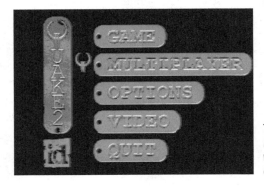

The Multiplayer option in Quake 2's menu is where you start a game or join a Network Server.

3. The Multiplayer menu offers three options. Use the arrow keys to select Start Network Server, and press Enter.

4. You'll see a screen with options for controlling the behavior of the game. If you like, you can change the default settings by using the arrow keys to move among options.

5. When you're finished setting options, use the down-arrow key to move to the Begin item at the bottom of the menu. Press Enter; players can now join the game from their computers.

Start a Quake Network Server by selecting the Begin item at the bottom of the Options screen.

Join a Multiplayer Game

With a Quake Network Server running on your network, players can join the game.

To join a multiplayer Quake game:

1. Start Quake and press Esc to get to the main Quake menu.

2. Press the arrow keys to select the Multiplayer option and then press Enter.

3. The Multiplayer menu displays three options. Choose Join Network Server and press Enter.

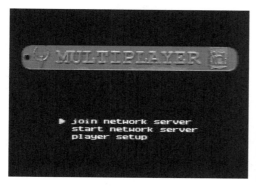

Join a multiplayer Quake game by selecting Join Network Server and hitting Enter.

4. In the next screen, you use the arrow keys to select the server on your network, and press Enter one last time to get in the game.

Star Wars: X-Wing Alliance

X-Wing Alliance is the third of the Star Wars games from LucasArts (*http://www.lucasarts.com/*) and is the most comprehensive multiplayer version. (The original X-Wing is single-player game.) A single-player game enmeshes you in a story set in the Star Wars world, where each mission advances the plot as if you were in the movie. In multiplayer mode you'll experience less of the overall plot, but you do have a choice of several types of games to play. In multiplayer skirmishes, players can choose to fly one of several ships, including one from the enemy Empire—something you can't do in single-player mode. Players can all attack a large Empire ship together or defend against an invasion. X-Wing Alliance also offers a multiplayer racing game, in which you compete against other players through the pilot proving grounds.

X-Wing Alliance uses either TCP/IP or IPX/SPX for a maximum of eight players on your network. (At press time, no Macintosh version of X-Wing Alliance was available, but Mac versions of the other X-Wing games do exist.) As with Quake, you need to set up one computer (called the "host" machine) as the X-Wing Alliance game server. This machine can be one of the players' computers, but you're more likely to get smoother game performance if the game host is a computer that no one is using.

Hire a Hefty Host: For the best game play, you should set up the game host on the fastest computer participating in the game. The faster the host computer, the smoother the game will be. LucasArts recommends that the host computer be a Pentium II PC or better with at least 64 MB of RAM.

The X-Wing Alliance games have been very popular, but LucasArts churns out a lot of different games based on the *Star Wars* movies. Some of those created after the X-Wing series include Star Wars: Episode 1 Racer, a racing game; and Star Wars: Episode 1—The Phantom Menace, an arcade-style game. Both are based on the fourth *Star Wars* film.

StarCraft

StarCraft and its sequel, StarCraft: Brood War, from Blizzard Entertainment are two of the top multiplayer strategy games. Up to eight people can participate on a local network; each player must develop a personal strategy while figuring out what the other players are up to.

You can also play StarCraft on the Internet through the Battle.net Web site at http://www.battle.net.

StarCraft features three species battling it out for control of the galaxy. Each player becomes a character in one of the three species. With more than two players, you can play cooperatively in teams. Multiplayer mode lets you choose from a dozen different game types, each with a different definition of what winning means, either for a team or an individual player.

StarCraft requires IPX/SPX protocol for PCs and Macs or AppleTalk for Mac-only networks; you can't use TCP/IP for games on your local network.

If you find that you aren't able to create a new multiplayer StarCraft game, you don't have the complete version of the game. You have what Blizzard Entertainment calls a "spawned version," which can only join already established multiplayer games.

Try it out: You can get a free demo version of StarCraft at Blizzard's Web site at *http://www.blizzard.com*.

NASCAR Racing

You'll find racing games for all kinds of sports. You can drive various types of vehicles, including motorcycles, airplanes, and spaceships (as in X-Wing Alliance). And you can even try ski racing from your keyboard. A good example of the genre is the realistic and popular **NASCAR Racing** from Papyrus, an auto-racing simulator for PCs and Macintosh. NASCAR Racing simulates cars and actual NASCAR tracks.

Papyrus offers several versions of the game, each with its own features. For instance, the 1999 Edition provides 35 different race tracks and both trucks and cars for you to drive.

NASCAR Racing supports up to eight players using the IPX/SPX network protocol. A free demo of a single-player version is available on the Papyrus Web site (*http://www.papy.com*). For technical support for NASCAR Racing, you can visit the Web site of the game's creator, Sierra Sports (*http://www.sierra.com/*).

When you step from the world of games back to reality, your network can help you interact with other network users as real people instead of as characters in a game. You do this with **messaging software**—a more sophisticated and very cool alternative to shouting at someone in another room. Messaging is like a written phone call. For example, you can type a message to your daughter down the hall and it instantly pops up on her computer screen. She can send an immediate message to you in reply.

Instant Messaging

Messaging on a small network is intended for brief notes such as "We need to leave for the ball game in 10 minutes." Your messages generally aren't saved and can't be sent if the recipient isn't available ("online"). Messaging doesn't replace e-mail; the messaging software usually doesn't have the extensive message-handling and spell-checking features of e-mail programs.

Messaging software is simple to set up and can be inexpensive or even free to acquire. You can find messaging software as a separate freeware or shareware utility, or it may be part of other network software you already have, including some of programs discussed in this book. For instance, both Timbuktu Pro and Meeting Maker, discussed later in this chapter, have instant messaging features.

HDS Messaging

HDS Messaging is a free instant messaging program for Windows. It's from Hard Drive Software (*http://www.hiddenman.com*), a company that sells other types of networking products, too. HDS Messaging works using any protocol on your system, and it requires that you have file sharing set up and active. HDS Messaging allows you to save messages.

You install HDS Messaging on each PC. On one PC that you designate as the messaging host, you will also create a shared folder to contain a list of network users. This PC must be running and connected to the network for messaging to work.

Setting Up HDS Messaging

Setting up HDS Messaging takes just a few minutes. First you establish the host PC, and then you designate the remaining PCs as clients.

To set up an HDS Messaging host:

1. On the host PC, create a shared folder (see Chapter 7).

2. Double-click the file hdsmsg.exe to install HDS Messaging and follow the directions on screen. If you're not sure where to find this file on your hard disk, locate it with the Windows Find command (from Start, select Find, and then select Files or Folders to display the Find dialog box).

3. Launch HDS Messaging (click Start, select Programs, select the HDS Messaging folder, and then select the HDS Messaging program). The program starts without displaying any windows.

4. In the Windows Taskbar, click the HDS Messaging button to display the program's main window.

5. From the Configure menu, choose Settings. In the dialog box that appears, do all of the following:

   - Specify the shared folder where the list of network users will reside. You can either type the folder's path or click the Browse button to select the folder from yet another dialog box.

   - Type your name in the My Username field.

   - Select the Autostart at Logon option.

Designate a shared folder to contain the network user list

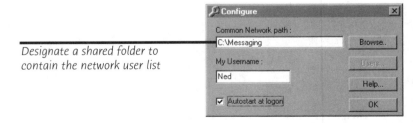

6. Click the OK button to close the Configure dialog box, and then open it again so you can add users with whom you'll exchange messages.

7. Click the User button to expand the Configure dialog box; you'll see a field for adding a name to a list of those who will use messaging. Type a name in this field and press the Enter key. Repeat for all network users you want to add to the list, including the user of the host PC. When you've entered all users, click OK to finish setting up the host.

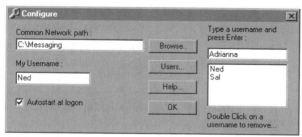

Add users to HDS Messaging by typing in their names.

To set up an HDS Messaging client:

1. Install and launch HDS Messaging as in steps 1 through 4 above. Open the Configure dialog box (in the Configure menu, choose Settings).

2. In the dialog box that appears, do all of the following:

- Type a name in the My Username field. This name must match one of the names entered on the host computer.

- Specify the path to the shared folder where the list of users resides on your network. Either type the path or click the Browse button to select it from another dialog box.

- Select the Autostart at Logon option.

3. Click OK to finish setup of the client.

When you launch HDS Messaging, it starts listening right away for messages from other network users, but it doesn't display its window until a message arrives. In the meantime, you can send a message by bringing up the HDS Messaging window yourself.

Sending a Message

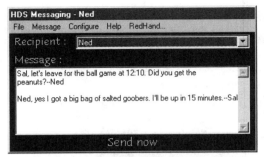

Ready to send a message with HDS Messaging.

To compose and send a message with HDS Messaging:

1. If the HDS Messaging window isn't already displayed, click the HDS Messaging button in the Taskbar.

2. Type a message.

3. In the Recipient field, click the arrow to drop down a list of user names. Select one.

4. Click Send. Your message will pop up on the recipient's screen in a matter of seconds, unless that user already has the Messaging window open. In this case, the recipient will receive your message after closing the window.

5. HDS Messaging asks if you want to send another message. Click Yes to send another message. If you click No, the window will disappear and the program will listen for incoming messages.

To receive and optionally reply to a message:

1. If the HDS Messaging window is open, close it. Incoming messages will not be displayed while the window is open.

2. When someone on the network sends you a message, the HDS Messaging window pops up to show you the incoming message. Read the message and decide whether to reply.

- If you want to reply, you can select the entire incoming message and type a replacement response, or you can type your message above or below the incoming message. In the latter case, leave a couple of blank lines or type a line of dashes to separate your reply, and put your name or initials at the end of your reply to differentiate it from the initial sent message. Continue at step 3 in the preceding procedure for sending a message.

- If you don't want to reply, choose Listen For New Messages from the Message menu. The HDS Messaging window closes, and you're ready to receive another message.

While all those ephemeral messages are shuttling across your network, you and other network users can share comparatively permanent information collected in **databases**. Storing information electronically using a database application enables you to find a piece of information quickly; that same application helps you sort and manage the data collection. By using the network to access a communal database file residing on one computer, everyone can share the same up-to-date collection of information.

Accessing Shared Databases

A database application may handle all kinds of information or it may specialize in one kind. A **general-purpose database application** lets you store just about any kind of information, such as invoices, recipes, or a catalog of your music collection. You define the structure and appearance of each database—perhaps based on templates provided with the database application—according to the kind of information the database will store. Microsoft Access and FileMaker Pro are two popular general-purpose database applications. In the upcoming section, you'll see how to use FileMaker Pro on your network.

General-Purpose Database Applications

You can also get a **specialized database program** that focuses on a particular type of data. For instance, a calendar program and an address book application are both specialized databases. The structure and appearance of a specialized database is usually predefined, although you may be able to customize it somewhat. In this chapter we'll take a look at the Meeting Maker group calendar and a group organizer called Eudora Planner.

Specialized Database Programs

The information in a database is stored in one or more files, so in theory you could use Windows or Macintosh file sharing to make the database files available on your network (as discussed in Chapter 7). In this case, any network computer could open the shared database files using its own copy of the database or calendar program. File sharing, however, may not permit more than one computer to open a particular file at the same time—a disadvantage to good utilization of the group's information.

No File Sharing

A **true multiuser database program** doesn't use Windows or Macintosh file sharing. Instead, a copy of the database program on one computer acts as a **host**, or server, for a database file. Additional copies of the database program on other computers then contact the host computer as **guests**, or clients, to get access to the shared database file. The host allows multiple network clients to have the same database file open simultaneously. Each user can view the information and make changes to it, but the database program allows only one client at a time to change any one of the information records that make up the database. When a user changes a record, other users see the change right away. They do not need to close and reopen the file.

Using FileMaker Pro

One of the easiest-to-use and easiest-to-network general-purpose database applications available for both Windows and Macintosh is **FileMaker Pro** from FileMaker, Inc. Each copy of FileMaker can host (serve) the database files that other network users access, and the same copy of FileMaker can access database files on other computers as a guest. FileMaker has the capability to network and to let multiple users access it without requiring file sharing.

In addition to the standard version of FileMaker Pro (which is multiuser), a special high-end version called **FileMaker Pro Server** provides faster access for up to 100 users. FileMaker Pro Server is meant to run on a dedicated server machine on a large network.

Try it out: If you'd like to take a look at FileMaker Pro, free trial versions of the software for both Windows and Macintosh are available at FileMaker, Inc.'s Web site (*http://www.filemaker.com*). The trial version doesn't work over a network, however, and it has other feature limitations as well, including one that prevents you from adding more than 50 records to a database.

FileMaker Pro can use several network protocols for communications. If your network has all Windows machines or a mixture of Windows and Macs, you can use TCP/IP or IPX/SPX with FileMaker Pro. An all-Mac network can also use AppleTalk. Of course, each computer on the network using FileMaker Pro must use the same protocol to communicate. The protocol you want to use must already be set up on the computers running FileMaker (see Chapter 3 for Windows setup and Chapter 4 for Macintosh setup).

Configuring FileMaker Pro for Network Use

To set the protocol, do the following on each computer that has FileMaker Pro:

1. In FileMaker Pro, from the Edit menu, select Preferences and then choose Application. This displays the General section of the Applications Preferences dialog box.

2. Choose a network protocol from the Network Protocol pop-up menu.

3. Click the Done button.

4. To make the protocol setting take effect, quit and restart FileMaker Pro.

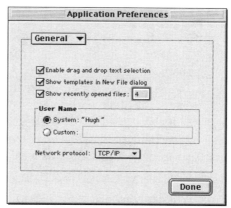

Designate the network protocol you want FileMaker Pro to use.

Sharing a FileMaker Pro Database

After you've designated the same network protocol on every computer that has FileMaker Pro, you can share a FileMaker Pro database. Network users with FileMaker Pro on their computers will be able to open your shared database file over the network, without using file sharing.

*The computer on which a shared FileMaker Pro database file resides is called a **host**—as it is for some games.*

To set up a FileMaker Pro database for multiuser access:

1. In FileMaker Pro, open the database file you want to share.

2. From the File menu, choose Sharing.

3. In the dialog box that appears, select the Multi-User option.

4. Click OK.

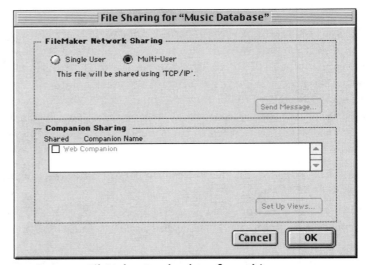

Setting up at FileMaker Pro database for multiuser access.

Defining Access Privileges in FileMaker Pro

FileMaker Pro lets you specify who can access a database. You can limit the actions other network users can take on the database, including browsing, printing, creating, editing, and deleting records. You can impose other restrictions, as well; FileMaker lets you limit users' ability to view or change individual fields. For example, in a database file containing customer contact information, you might not want temporary workers to have access to customers' home phone numbers. In that case, you could use access privileges to "hide" those fields.

To set access privileges for a multiuser database file:

1. Open the database file you are sharing. From the File menu, select Access Privileges and then choose Define Groups.

2. In the Group Name field of the Define Groups dialog box, type a new group name. Click the Create button, and the new group name will show up in the list on the left. You can add more groups by typing their names and clicking Create.

3. To create a password for a group, select the group name from the list and click the Passwords button.

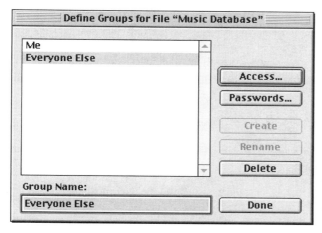

Each group you define can get access to different parts of a FileMaker Pro database.

4. In the Define Passwords dialog box, type a password and then click the Create button.

Adding a Password

5. Click the Access button to open the Access Privileges dialog box.

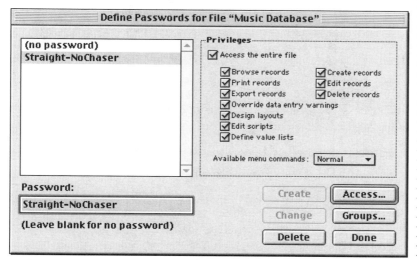

Assigning privileges to each password you create for a FileMaker Pro database.

6. In the Access Privileges dialog box, click a group in the Groups column.

7. In the Passwords column, click the circles next to the passwords to darken the circles for the passwords you want the selected group to use.

8. You can now limit the group's access to database layouts and fields by clicking the circles next to the layout and field names. One click gives the group read-only access. A second click disables the group from seeing the layout or field. A third click restores full access.

9. Click Done to close the Access Privileges dialog box, and then click Done again to close the Passwords dialog box.

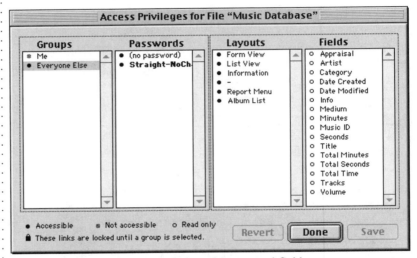

Limiting a group's access to database layouts and fields.

Opening a Database from Another Computer

*A computer that opens a shared FileMaker database residing on another computer is called a **guest**.*

After a FileMaker database file has been made shared and optionally had access privileges set for it, network users can open it from their computers over the network.

To open a database file on another computer:

1. Start FileMaker Pro on your computer and choose Open from the File menu.

2. Click the Hosts button in the Open dialog box. FileMaker Pro will search the network for multiuser databases that are open on other computers and display a list of them in another dialog box.

Opening a multiuser database hosted by FileMaker Pro on another computer in the network.

3. Select the name of the database file you want to open and click Open.

4. If the database is password-protected, a password dialog will appear. Type in the password.

The most common type of specialized database program organizes your **calendar** of appointments and your personal **contacts**. This type of program serves as an electronic version of a datebook and an address book. The multiuser, network variety of these programs are often called **group organizers**. Most group organizers also let you keep some private calendar and contact information to which other people don't have access. The calendar and contact information may be managed by one organizer program or by two programs that are linked together.

As for general-purpose databases, you could simply place a single-user organizer file in a shared folder, but then only one user would be able to access it at a time.

Meeting Maker from On Technology is a group calendar and scheduling program that has been around for a number of years. In addition to scheduling appointments and meetings, Meeting Maker lets you schedule meeting rooms. The software can use the TCP/IP or IPX/SPX protocol on Windows and TCP/IP, IPX/SPX, or AppleTalk on Macintosh.

Meeting Maker has two pieces: the server software, which is loaded on the computer hosting the data; and the client software, which is loaded on the other computers in the nework. If you're running the server software on your computer, you load the Meeting Maker client on the same computer to access the data.

Meeting Maker can also synchronize schedules with 3Com Palm handheld organizers.

Group Calendars and Organizers

Meeting Maker from On Technology

Try it out: Both the client and server software are available for Windows and Macintosh, and a trial version of the entire program can be downloaded from the Meeting Maker Web site at *http://www.meetingmaker6.com.*

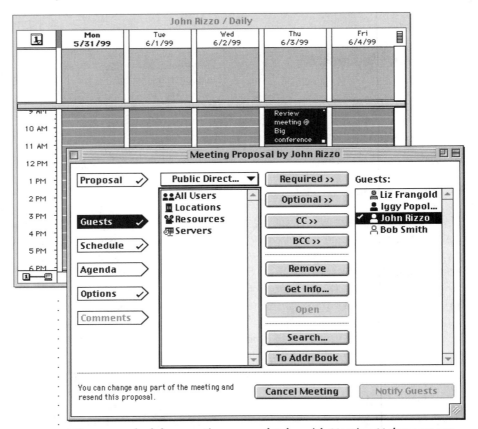

When you schedule a meeting on a calendar with Meeting Maker, you can invite other users. They'll get a message and can reply.

Meeting Maker works a little differently from other network databases. Schedules reside on the computer with the server software and are copied to each client computer when a user accesses the Meeting Maker server. This lets each user work offline, so that the computer with the server software on it doesn't have to be on all the time (as is the case with FileMaker Pro, for instance). Each time the user connects to the server software, the user's local schedule is synchronized with the central schedule on the server.

Meeting Maker also has a form of instant messaging called "real-time scheduling." When you invite other users to meetings via this messaging, a message pops up on the other users' screens asking if they can attend the meeting. The users can then either accept or reject the proposed meeting by clicking a button. If a user already has a scheduled appointment at that time, Meeting Maker will let you know immediately with a message.

Invite Others to Meetings

Qualcomm's **Eudora Planner** began its history as the popular duo, Now Up-to-Date and Now Contact. Qualcomm acquired the product, made some improvements, and reissued the software for Windows as Eudora Planner.

Eudora Planner

The Eudora Planner software uses the TCP/IP protocol for network communications. It can also synchronize data with the 3Com Palm computers and compatibles.

> At the time of this writing, Qualcomm had not released a Macintosh version of Eudora Planner, although a pre-release (*beta*) version has been available for more than a year. Qualcomm told us it was still planning to issue a complete Mac version with a set of features similar to the Windows version but could not provide a release date.

Eudora Planner is similar in many ways to Meeting Maker. It includes a host version called **Eudora Planner Server**, which you must buy in a package called **Eudora Group Planner**. (Eudora Group Planner also comes with five- or ten-client versions of the software for your other computers.) You install the Server program on one of the computers, and all of the users access it via copies of Eudora Planner. Qualcomm recommends that the Server machine be a computer dedicated to the task; it's not required, but you'll get better performance. The Server computer must also be configured with a static IP address. Unlike Meeting Maker, the Eudora Planner Server must be running at all times.

When you are connected to Eudora Planner Server over the network, you can selectively share calendars, contacts, and to-do lists. Each user can create information that is either public or private. You do this by setting up public or private "categories" and then assigning them to appointments, contacts, and to-do lists. Like Meeting Maker, Eudora Group Planner lets you invite users to meetings with a message that pops up on their screens. Each user can accept or decline the meeting.

Eudora Planner's Features

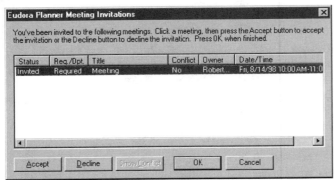

Eudora sends you this message when someone invites you to a meeting.

Try it out: Qualcomm offers demonstration versions of Eudora Planner for Windows at its Web site at *http://eudora.qualcomm.com/*.

File Backup

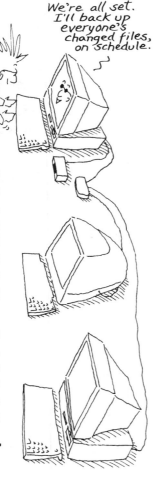

Backing up files is important to ensure against loss of your files because of hardware problems, power outages or spikes, or accidental deletion. Of course, you don't need a network to back up your files—anyone can copy important files to a Zip disk or tape cartridge. But a network backup operation goes one better: It lets you **centralize** and to some degree **automate** the backup of all the computers on the network. This makes backup a network service rather than an individual responsibility. Also, it's easier to manage the backup data from various computers when it is all collected by one computer. A smart backup program can recognize files that are identical on more than one computer and save time and space by saving only one copy on the backup device.

One backup strategy is for everyone to back up data to the same computer on the network. That is, everyone copies important data to the same shared disk on one of the computers by dragging files in the Windows Explorer or the Macintosh Finder. Then you back up that shared disk to **removable media**, such as tape or Zip cartridges, using any backup program that will run on the shared computer.

Don't overlook your **notebook computers** when it comes time to back up your data! The more a computer is moved around, the more prone it is to crashes and misfires. That notebook may not always be connected to the network, but you should make a point of connecting it for backup whenever possible.

Backup Media

You can use a network to back up files from several computers onto the hard disk of a single computer. However, we don't recommend storing the backup data on a computer's hard disk. For one thing, this data typically takes up substantial space, especially if you're backing up several computers' data. And if the backup computer is commonly used for work or play, it is more susceptible to problems and failures. So it's best to move the backup data to one of the **removable media types** listed in the table that follows.

Although backing up to a shared disk or shared folder on one network computer is less than ideal, it's better than no backup at all and more convenient than backing up to floppies, which don't hold much data. So you might consider one computer's hard disk as a stop-gap measure just until you get some sort of removable storage.

Media	Capacity	Cost	Comments
Tape	Medium to high	Low	DAT and QIC tape formats are good for small network backup. DAT tapes cost less than QIC tapes, but DAT drives cost more that QIC drives. Retrieving individual files takes considerable time.
Zip disk	Low	High	Comparatively unreliable. A complete network backup requires an impractical number of Zip disks.
Jaz disk	Medium	Medium	Provides quick retrieval of individual files.
Optical	Medium to high	Low	Safest for long-term archiving. Media include CD-R, CD-RW, DVD-RAM, and magneto-optical.
Internet	Low to medium	Medium	Off-site storage provides extra safety in the event of a natural disaster. Success/affordability depends on performance and reliability of Internet connection.

Short-Term Backup vs. Long-Term Archiving

Short-term backup and long-term archiving are two similar activities done for different purposes. A **short-term backup** saves an extra copy of your work at a particular point in time—this is handy for safeguarding unfinished work. You can use the backup to **restore** your work in case of a problem or in case you need to see an earlier version of your work. Short-term backup has a practical shelf life of a few weeks or months. **A long-term archive** saves finished work that you want to keep around for a long time. Some backup media are better suited to short-term backup; others make more sense for long-term archiving.

Software for Your Backup

Although you can always back up a few essential files by manually dragging them to a shared disk, backup utility software is more convenient, thorough, and efficient. A **backup utility** backs up only the files that have changed since the last backup was completed. This **incremental backup** saves time and space on the backup media. Even more space is saved when the utility compresses what it's backing up.

The problem with most network backup software, especially for Windows PCs, is that it usually requires a dedicated server computer. In addition, these backup programs can cost big bucks. The popular and full-featured ARCserve from Computer Associates sells for well over $1000, for instance.

Alternatives for a Small Network

Since you probably don't have a dedicated server on your small network, we'll discuss some alternatives here. First we'll look at Retrospect, a unique network backup utility that doesn't require a server and serves both PC and Mac networks. NovaBackup and Seagate Backup Exec, which are designed for backing up a single Windows PC, can also partially back up the shared disks of other network PCs.

Retrospect

Whether your network includes Windows PCs, Macintosh computers, or both, **Retrospect** from Dantz Development Corp. is our first choice for network backup. It's affordable for home and small office use, and it doesn't require a dedicated server. You can schedule automatic backups for convenient times, and each user can decide when to back up.

Retrospect backs up not only the hard disks of any or all computers on the network but also removable disks that are inserted at the time of backup. The utility finds all the disks to be backed up, without using Windows or Macintosh file sharing. Retrospect can back up to a variety of media, including tape, Zip and Jaz, and optical disks. You can also back up to an Internet site. Retrospect uses the TCP/IP protocol to communicate with Windows and Macintosh computers, or it can use the AppleTalk protocol on a Mac-only network.

You can even set up Retrospect to back up notebook computers as soon as they are connected to the network. Practically speaking, this capability requires Retrospect to be running all the time (on the computer with the tape drive or other backup device) so it can tell when a notebook is connected to the network.

The main Retrospect application runs on the network computer with a tape drive or another backup device. This main application communicates with small Retrospect client programs installed on the other computers in the network.

Setting up the Retrospect application is straightforward. After installing the software, you use a feature called **EasyScript** to set up a backup schedule. EasyScript asks you how often you want to back up, which computers to back up, and other relevant questions. Then it creates the backup schedule for you. At each appointed backup time, Retrospect launches and performs the backup. All you have to do is remember to leave the computers turned on; you can set up Retrospect to shut each machine down after backup is completed.

Try it out: To try out a demo version of Retrospect, go to Dantz's Web site at *http://www.dantz.com*.

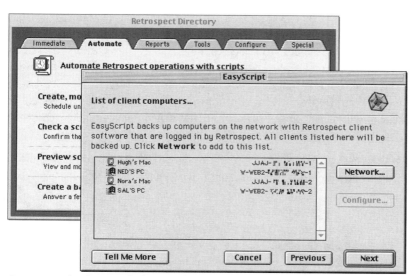

Retrospect backs up Windows and Macintosh computers over the network.

NovaBackup

NovaBackup from NovaStor is a low-cost (under $100) backup utility for Windows. (The current version is not available for Macintosh.) NovaBackup 6.0 comes with two utilities: NovaBack for backing up to a wide variety of tape drives, and NovaDisk for backing up to removable disks. NovaBackup can also compress data before storing it on your media.

NovaBackup isn't designed specifically for network backup (although a version for a dedicated Windows NT Server is available). But like some other backup utilities, NovaBackup can be fooled into backing up the hard drives of other PCs by using Windows file sharing. Unlike Retrospect, however, NovaBackup won't back up a PC's Registry over a network, and the backup process isn't as automated as it is with Retrospect. NovaBackup is a cheaper solution than Retrospect because the software needs to be running on only one PC.

NovaBackup puts file sharing to work.

To use NovaBackup on a network, you first turn on file sharing for all the PCs and share each PC's entire hard disk with full access (not just read-only access). (Chapter 7 explains how to do this.) On the PC running NovaBackup, you connect to all the shared disks and map each one to a drive letter (as described in Chapter 8). If you don't map the shared disks as network drives, NovaBackup can't back them up. Once this is done, you can copy the files to a tape or removable disk.

Setting up NovaBackup is easy to figure out but requires a little more work than Retrospect. You need to tell the software whether to back up every file on a PC's hard drive or to do an incremental backup of files that have changed since a particular date. Fortunately, you can save multiple configurations for running later. (Just press the Save Procedure button and name the setup.) You can also schedule NovaBackup to run at convenient times.

Try it out: If you'd like to try out NovaBackup, you can download a demo copy of the software from (*http://www.novastor.com/*).

Seagate Backup Exec

Not every single-user Windows backup utility can back up network drives mapped to drive letters, nor is NovaBackup the only one that can. **Seagate Backup Exec** is another low-cost utility that lets you back up to a variety of tape media, magnetic and optical removable disks, and hard drives.

Like NovaBackup, Seagate Backup Exec backs up the Windows Registry only for the machine that it's running on. On a local machine, a single-button feature called Integrated Emergency Recovery rebuilds Windows and all of the various configuration files as they were previously configured, so you don't have to reinstall Windows and all your other software. This feature does not work on computers over the network. Seagate Backup Exec, however, comes in versions for various types of dedicated servers; these versions do backup and restore the low-level configuration information for all network computers.

Try it out: You can get a demo version of Seagate Backup Exec at the Seagate Software Web site (*http://www.seagatesoftware.com*).

You can remotely control a television and a stereo—why not a computer? Well, actually, you can do this—except, instead of using a little plastic keypad, you use another computer. And a network, of course.

So why would you want to control one computer from another? There are lots of reasons. You might want to run software installed on one computer that isn't installed on another computer. Maybe your computer is too old to run the latest software, or you don't have enough memory, or maybe the software you want to run is not available for your operating system. You can use **remote control software** to do the following:

- Run software that resides on another computer in your network.

- Operate hardware connected to another computer, such as a modem, a printer, or a DVD drive. This is another way to share peripherals among the computers on your network.

- Configure other computers on your network without getting up from your desk.

- Allow other computer users to watch what you are doing on your computer. This lets you use the software to conduct a training session, for example.

Additionally, remote control software doesn't stop with remote control. It usually offers other features that take advantage of your network, such as messaging and enhanced file transfer.

Netopia's **Timbuktu Pro** is the only remote control product that works with both Windows and Macintosh. This program enables a Windows user to run Mac software while sitting at a PC, and it lets a Mac user run Windows software while operating a Macintosh. (Of course, Timbuktu works with all-Windows or all-Mac networks as well.) You can use Timbuktu Pro to control another computer or to just watch what's

Controlling Another Computer

Timbuktu Pro

happening on that computer. Timbuktu offers a bunch of other useful features as well.

Every computer that is to participate in remote control must be running a copy of Timbuktu Pro. The software uses TCP/IP for Windows and Macintosh, and the Macintosh version can also use AppleTalk to control or view other Macs.

Try it out: Netopia offers limited demo versions of Timbuktu for Windows and Macintosh at its Web site (*http://www.netopia.com*). The demo software works over a network, but some of its features are not available or scaled back.

Timbuktu Pro for Macintosh can allow multiple Mac and Windows users to view a single Mac's operation simultaneously. However, the Windows version allows only one viewer at a time.

Timbuktu Basics

To enable other Timbuktu Pro users to control or view your computer, choose **Visitor Privileges** from the Setup menu. If you're going to allow users to access your computer without a password, double-click the **Public Visitor** item in the Visitor Privileges window. To add an individual **Trusted Visitor**, who must enter a password to connect to your computer, double-click the **Ask for Permission** item. Double-clicking an item listed in the Visitor Privileges window displays a Visitor dialog box for that item.

Identify users who can access your computer in Timbuktu Pro.

In the Visitor dialog box, choose options that determine what the visitor is allowed to do on your computer. The Public Visitor dialog box determines privileges for all Timbuktu users who connect to your computer without a password. The Trusted Visitor dialog box affects only the one visitor—you can configure privileges differently for each Trusted Visitor, if you like.

In the Visitor dialog box, you can determine what a network user can do on your computer.

Users can **start a Timbuktu session** in several ways. Windows and Macintosh users both can use the New Connection window, accessed from Timbuktu's File menu, to see a list of other Timbuktu computers on the network and create a remote control session with one of them. Windows users can look through the Network Neighborhood, right-click a PC with Timbuktu, and use the shortcut menu to make a new remote-control session. Also, both Windows and Mac users can use Timbuktu to create desktop icons for computers they'd like to control on a regular basis.

Timbuktu Pro is more than a remote-control program. You can use it to perform **fast file transfers**, even between Windows and Macintosh computers. This feature can be handy if you're working with software running on another computer and want to save the resulting file to your computer for safekeeping but don't have cross-platform file sharing set up.

You can also **send messages** to other Timbuktu users. Messages arrive in a folder called Messages Received. You can reply to and forward messages.

If messaging is too slow, you can create a **real-time chat** session among users. A Timbuktu Pro chat session looks a lot like Internet-based chat sessions, with messages and responses scrolling by as each person posts them.

Other Timbuktu Pro Features

And if you'd rather be vocal, you can use Timbuktu as a **voiced-based intercom system**. This feature is useful when someone is viewing your computer during an instructional session.

Timbuktu Pro has built-in messaging.

pcAnywhere

The **pcAnywhere** product from Symantec is not quite as full-featured as Timbuktu Pro (it lacks the voice messaging feature). It also doesn't support the Mac OS. Symantec does have a Windows CE version, however, which lets you control some hand-held computers from a PC.

Try it out: You can download a 30-day trial version of pcAnywhere from Symantec's Web site (*http://www.symantec.com*).

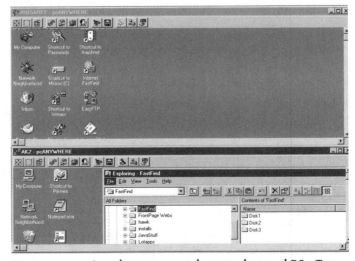

You can use pcAnywhere to remotely control several PCs: Two remote control sessions are shown here.

Summary

You can extend the functionality of your network by purchasing and installing additional software.

▼ In **multiplayer games**, you can match wits and skill with other human players rather than with the computer.

▼ **Messaging** software is like a written phone call—an alternative to shouting at someone in another room.

▼ A **multiuser database** application lets network users share the same up-to-date collection of information. The database may be general purpose or specialized.

▼ A **network backup** provides insurance for your whole network against loss of files due to hardware or power problems or accidental file deletion.

▼ With **remote control** software, you can use software and hardware on other network computers. You can also configure other computers and run a training session for other users working on different computers.

Part Three

Appendix & Glossary

Troubleshoot Your Network

When you have trouble with your network, you can consult this appendix, which lists a variety of common networking problems and offers solutions for fixing them. The problems are arranged in several categories as follows:

- Windows Networking Troubleshooter
- Windows Network Setup Problems
- Window File and Printer Sharing Problems
- Internet Sharing Problems
- Macintosh Printer Sharing Problems
- Macintosh File Sharing Problems
- Macintosh Network Setup Problems

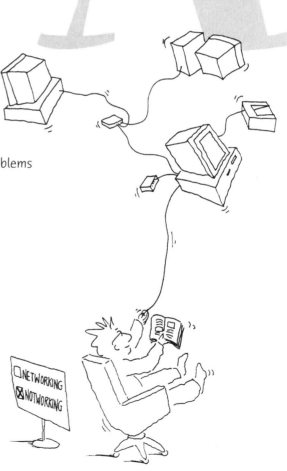

Windows Networking Troubleshooter

Both Windows 95 and Windows 98 include **interactive network troubleshooting** as part of their on-screen help systems. The troubleshooters stick close to the real-world problems that have come up most often in sessions with Microsoft's Windows telephone support technicians. As you might expect, Windows 98 troubleshooting is a bit more extensive than that for the earlier version of the operating system.

To start the Windows Networking Troubleshooter:

1. From the Start menu, choose Help.

2. In the Index tab, scroll down to networks, and then double-click troubleshooting.

3. Windows 98 users: Click the underlined text "Click here" on the right side of the Help window to display the Networking Troubleshooter in the Help window.

  Windows 95 users: The Network Troubleshooter appears in a new window.

4. Follow the instructions on screen.

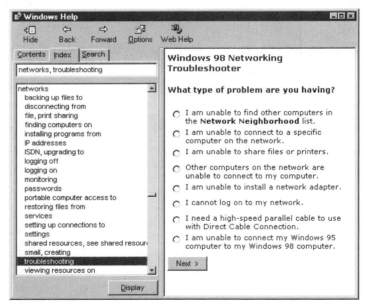

The Windows Networking Troubleshooter interactively helps you solve your networking problems.

Plug and Play detects wrong network adapter.

The first time you start up a PC after installing a Plug and Play-compatible network adapter, Windows detects the new hardware and installs the driver software for it. If Windows doesn't recognize the type of adapter, Windows may install the wrong driver software. In this case, you need to install the correct driver software using the disk that came with the adapter. (See Chapter 2.)

Windows doesn't notice a new network adapter.

Make sure the card is installed in the right type of slot. PCI slots are shorter in length than ISA slots.

Also, check the computer's specifications to make sure its PCI slots support bus mastering. Some computers support bus mastering on only one PCI slot.

While installing an adapter card, a message reports an IRQ conflict.

An IRQ (interrupt request line) is a communications hotline between a device such as a network adapter and the CPU. A conflict occurs when two devices contend for the same IRQ. Windows 95 and 98 will resolve IRQ conflicts between Plug and Play devices, but if your PC is loaded with devices or has any old devices that are not Plug and Play, you may encounter IRQ conflicts. For help resolving conflicts, contact the manufacturers of the PC, the network adapter card, and other expansion cards.

The link light on the hub does not come on.

▼ Make sure the hub is switched on; ditto the computer.

▼ Make sure the cable is plugged into a numbered port on the hub, not into a port labeled Uplink. If the hub has a switch labeled Uplink, make sure it is in the Normal or Off position. (The Uplink switch changes the internal wiring of one port on the hub, generally the highest-numbered port, to enable linking hubs.)

▼ Test the hub by taking a cable from a computer that you know works and plugging it into the suspect port on the hub. If the hub port's link light comes on, you know the hub port is working.

▼ Test the computer's network port by connecting it to a known good hub port with a pre-tested Ethernet cable. If necessary, you can temporarily move the hub near the computer.

Windows Network Setup Problems

- *If the link light comes on when you use a pre-tested Ethernet cable,* there is a problem with the regular wiring between the computer and the hub. Review the wiring instructions in Chapter 2.

- *If the link light does not come on when you use a pre-tested Ethernet cable,* there is a problem with the computer's Ethernet hardware. Make sure the network adapter is installed correctly, as described in Chapter 2 and according to the manufacturer's directions. Make sure any switches on the card are properly set.

- *If the computer has a network adapter with more than one type of connector,* such as an RJ-45 connector for 10BaseT or 10/100BaseT and a BNC connector for thinnet, check the adapter's documentation. Look for instructions about how to set the adapter to use the RJ-45 connector.

The computer seems to take longer to start up than before you set up your network.

IP address search: If Windows 98 is set to assign itself an IP address (as described in Chapter 3), you may notice a delay during startup while Windows looks for a DHCP server to provide an IP address. Your small network probably doesn't have a DHCP server unless you have an Internet gateway that includes one, and Windows eventually stops looking and assigns itself an IP address.

Dual-speed systems: You may notice a delay when starting up a computer with a 10/100BaseT port that is connected to a 10/100BaseT hub. It may take a little extra time for the dual-speed port and dual-speed hub to negotiate the best speed.

TCP/IP applications don't work.

If one or more of your computers seems unable to use any network services, the TCP/IP configuration may be incorrect on the affected computers. Check these items:

- Make sure each computer has a unique IP address.
- Make sure each computer has the same subnet mask.

Also, review the configuration instructions in Chapter 3.

If you installed an Internet gateway as described in Chapter 5, review the configuration instructions included with the gateway product.

A computer on the network doesn't appear in your Network Neighborhood.

▼ In the Network Neighborhood double-click the Entire Network icon. If you still don't see an icon for the computer to which you want to connect, double-click the icon that represents your workgroup.

(If the Entire Network icon is not present, the network software is not installed correctly; review Chapter 3.)

▼ Make sure the computer that you want to connect to is turned on.

▼ Check the configuration of the Network dialog box on the computer to which you want to connect.

   ▪ In the Configuration tab, make sure the Client for Windows Network item is in the list of installed network components (see Chapter 3). Click the File and Print Sharing button and make sure the check boxes are set correctly (see Chapters 6 and 7).

   ▪ In the Access Control tab, make sure share-level access control is selected.

   ▪ In the Identification tab, make sure that the Workgroup entry is the same for every computer and that the Computer Name entry is different for every computer.

▼ Confirm that your computer and the computer to which you want to connect are using the same protocol. One or more of these protocols should be listed at the top of the Configuration tab in the Network dialog box of both computers: TCP/IP, NetBEUI, or IPX/SPX. Add any missing protocols and remove any unneeded protocols as described in Chapter 3.

The computer to which you want to connect doesn't recognize your password.

▼ Confirm the spelling of your password.

▼ Check with the user of the other computer to see if the password has been changed.

A shared printer doesn't appear in the Network Neighborhood.

▼ On the host computer, right-click the printer's icon, choose Sharing from the shortcut menu, and make sure the printer is set to be shared.

▼ If the printer connects directly to the network (not directly to a computer), make sure the printer is turned on and ready to print.

Windows File and Printer Sharing Problems

After installing a shared printer in your Printers folder, you can't print to it.

▼ Check to see if the printer is turned on and ready to print.

▼ If the printer is connected to a computer, make sure that computer is turned on.

▼ Some printers can't be shared. Check with the printer manufacturer about your printer model.

Shared folders or disks you want to access don't appear in the Network Neighborhood.

▼ On the host computer, right-click the folder or disk icon, choose Sharing from the shortcut menu, and make sure the folder or disk is set to be shared.

▼ On the host computer, right-click the icon for the folder or disk, choose Sharing from shortcut menu, and see if the share name has a dollar sign ($) at the end. If you see the $, this item won't show up in the Network Neighborhood. You can, however, connect to it by typing its network path.

When you copy files or print, the network is busy or the resource is unavailable.

When many activities are occurring simultaneously on the network (copying files, printing, browsing the Internet, and/or playing multi-player games) the network can become overloaded and some computers will be unable to communicate (usually the ones farthest apart). You may get a message to this effect. Wait a few minutes for activity to subside on the network, and then try again.

Internet Sharing Problems

Your first attempted Web connection fails, but the second attempt works.

Here's how this could happen: The first time you try to go to a Web site, your network's Internet gateway is not yet connected to your ISP. While the connection process is underway, your Web browser looks for a DNS server to translate the Web site's URL into an IP address. The browser's internal timer tells it to stop looking before the ISP's DNS server is able to respond, and the browser reports it cannot find the Web site. You try again to go to the Web site, and this time the gateway is connected to the ISP; the DNS server responds to the Web browser's request.

You can make the Web browser spend more time looking for a DNS server by listing more DNS server addresses. The additional addresses can be duplicates of addresses that are already listed. For example, if the two addresses 205.166.226.38 and 208.146.254.90 are listed, simply list the same two addresses again. Follow the instructions included with your Internet gateway for specifying DNS server addresses.

None of your Internet applications can successfully connect.

If other network computers can connect but yours can't, your computer's IP address or gateway address may be incorrect. Make sure TCP/IP is configured according to the instructions for your Internet gateway.

Your Web browser can't find any Web sites.

The DNS addresses may be set incorrectly. Here are a couple of solutions:

- Try connecting to a Web site by typing its IP address in the Location or Address box at the top of the Web browser window and then pressing Enter or Return. For example, type **http://207.149.188.79** and press Enter or Return to connect to the Peachpit Web site.

- If this works, check to make sure DNS addresses are entered according to the instructions for your Internet gateway. For example, if your Internet gateway uses NAT (see Chapter 5), you generally must enter your ISP's DNS addresses on each computer.

Or, your ISP may be experiencing a temporary service disruption.

Your Mac's shared Internet connection's modem or ISDN modem dials unexpectedly.

On a Mac with Mac OS 8.6 and earlier, make sure the TCP/IP control panel is configured for your local network and not for a PPP connection to the Internet. If you created one named configuration for your local network and another for a PPP connection to the Internet, as described in Chapter 4, make sure the configuration for the local network is active. To confirm the configuration, open the TCP/IP control panel and then press Command-K.

Macintosh Printer Sharing Problems

The link light on the hub does not come on.

▼ Make sure the hub is switched on; ditto the computer.

▼ Make sure the cable is plugged into a numbered port on the hub, not into a port labeled Uplink. If the hub has a switch labeled Uplink, make sure it is in the Normal or Off position. (The Uplink switch changes the internal wiring of one port on the hub, generally the highest-numbered port, to enable linking hubs.)

▼ Test the hub by taking a cable from a computer that you know works and plugging it into the suspect port on the hub. If the hub port's link light comes on, you know the hub port is working.

▼ Test the computer's network port by connecting it to a known good hub port with a pre-tested Ethernet cable. If necessary, you can temporarily move the hub near the computer.

  ▪ *If the link light comes on when you use a pre-tested Ethernet cable*, there is a problem with the regular wiring between the computer and the hub. Review the wiring instructions in Chapter 2.

  ▪ *If the link light does not come on when you use a pre-tested Ethernet cable*, there is a problem with the computer's Ethernet hardware. Make sure the network adapter is installed correctly, as described in Chapter 2 and according to the manufacturer's directions. Make sure any switches on the card are properly set.

  ▪ *If the computer has a network adapter with more than one type of connector*, such as an RJ-45 connector for 10BaseT or 10/100BaseT and a BNC connector for thinnet, check the adapter's documentation. Look for instructions about how to set the adapter to use the RJ-45 connector.

The computer seems to take longer to start up than before you set up your network.

You may notice a delay when starting up a computer with a 10/100BaseT port that is connected to a 10/100BaseT hub. It may take a little extra time for the dual-speed port and dual-speed hub to negotiate the best speed.

The computer locks up for about 15 seconds every 5 or 10 minutes.

If Mac OS 8.5–8.6 is set to assign itself an IP address (as described in Chapter 4), it will assign itself a new IP address every 5 or 10 minutes. During this process, the Mac OS may lock up the computer for several seconds while it looks for a DHCP server in case one has become available on your network. Your small network probably doesn't have a DHCP server, unless you have an Internet gateway that includes one. So the Mac OS eventually stops looking and assigns itself an IP address. You can eliminate the problem by assigning IP addresses manually, as described in Chapter 4.

Your computer can't use any network services.

If the network is connected to the Mac's built-in Ethernet port, make sure the Ethernet driver is installed. Go to the AppleTalk control panel and check the Connect Via pop-up menu. If the menu doesn't include any Ethernet choices, the Ethernet driver is not installed. You can install the standard Ethernet driver by doing a custom installation with the Mac OS installer program. Specify that you want the network software component to be installed.

If the network is connected to an Ethernet adapter (a PC card on a PowerBook or an internal expansion card on a desktop Mac), make sure the latest driver software for the adapter is installed in the Extensions folder inside the System folder. Check the Web site of the adapter's manufacturer for updated driver software, and install it. If no driver installation disk was packaged with the network adapter hardware, the network adapter probably uses the standard driver provided with the Mac OS (see the preceding paragraph).

TCP/IP applications don't work.

If one or more of your computers seems unable to use any network services except shared printers and file sharing, the TCP/IP configuration may be incorrect on the affected computers. Check these items in the TCP/IP control panel:

- Make sure each computer has a unique IP address.
- Make sure each computer has the same subnet mask.
- Set the TCP/IP control panel to Advanced mode (from the Edit menu, choose User Mode), and make sure the option Use 802.3 is turned off.

Also, review the Mac configuration instructions in Chapter 4.

If you installed an Internet gateway as described in Chapter 5, review the configuration instructions included with the gateway product.

You can't remember your Administrator password.

The AppleTalk, Modem, PPP, Remote Access, and TCP/IP control panels have an Administration mode that you won't need to use on a small network. If for some reason you *have* used Administration mode and you entered a password but have now forgotten it, you can erase the password along with all the control panel settings. To do this, drag the AppleTalk Preferences, Modem Preferences, Remote Access Preferences, or TCP/IP Preferences file out of the Preferences folder and restart the Mac.

Macintosh Network Setup Problems

The printer icon doesn't appear on the left side of the Chooser.

▼ If the printer is a PostScript printer, its icon may not be displayed in the Chooser. Try using the LaserWriter 8 icon.

▼ Make sure the printer driver file is not disabled in the Extensions Manager control panel (or in Conflict Catcher, if you use it instead).

▼ If the printer driver file is not listed in the Extensions Manager at all, make sure the printer driver file is not "loose" in the System Folder; it should be located in the Extensions folder. If the printer driver file is nowhere to be found, you need to install the printer driver software, as described in Chapter 6.

▼ The printer driver software may be defective. You can replace it by re-installing the Printing component of the Mac OS or by installing the latest driver distributed by the printer's manufacturer.

▼ If the printer driver file is in the Extensions folder and its filename includes the extension .sea, .sit, .hqx, .smi, .img, .cpt, or .bin, it has not been properly installed. All these filename suffixes indicate the file is compressed or encoded, perhaps for Internet delivery. Try dragging the file to the desktop and double-clicking it to expand and decode it.

After clicking the printer icon in the Chooser, the printer isn't listed on the right side of the Chooser.

▼ Make sure the printer is turned on and ready to print. If it's a shared local printer, make sure the printer's computer is also turned on.

▼ Make sure the AppleTalk option is set to Active in the Chooser on your computer and on the computer whose printer you want to use.

▼ Make sure the Connect Via option in the AppleTalk control panel is set to the correct port, as described in Chapter 4.

▼ If you are using Mac OS 8.5 or later and the printer is configured for TCP/IP printing instead of AppleTalk, the printer will not appear in the Chooser. The details of using a TCP/IP printer are beyond the scope of this book. Refer to the Mac OS Help system.

A printer appears and disappears in the Chooser.

Check the wiring that goes to the printer for loose connections, damaged cables, and proximity to fluorescent lights and other sources of electromagnetic interference.

On a LocalTalk network, check for proper termination, and make sure the daisy-chain is not a closed loop, as described in Chapter 2.

The Chooser or Network Browser doesn't list the computer to which you want to connect.

▼ Make sure the computer that you want to connect to is turned on.

▼ On the computer that you want to connect to, open the File Sharing control panel or Sharing Setup control panel, and make sure file sharing is active.

▼ If you're using the Chooser (not the Network Browser) on your computer, make sure you have clicked the AppleShare icon.

▼ Make sure the AppleTalk option is set to Active in the Chooser on your computer and on the computer you want to connect to.

▼ Check the Connect Via setting in the AppleTalk control panel on your Mac and the Mac to which you want to connect. It must be set to the port where the network connects to the computer, as described in Chapter 2.

The Guest option is disabled (dimmed).

This means the computer you're trying to connect to doesn't allow guests to connect. (This is controlled by the Guest icon in the Users & Groups control panel on the computer to which you want to connect, as described in Chapter 7.)

The computer you want to connect to doesn't recognize your name or password.

▼ Make sure the Caps Lock key is not on.

▼ Confirm the spelling of your name with the person who uses the computer to which you want to connect. (Capitalization doesn't matter.)

▼ Confirm the spelling and capitalization of your password.

Macintosh File Sharing Problems

The Chooser or Network Browser does not list the shared folder or disk you want to use.

▼ The owner of the shared item may not have granted you permission you to see the item.

▼ The item you want to use may not be designated a shared item, as described in Chapter 7.

A shared folder or disk is dimmed in the Chooser's list of available shared items.

▼ You may already be connected to the shared item. Look for its icon on your desktop.

▼ The owner of the shared item may not have granted you permission to use it.

A shared folder or disk appears and disappears in the Chooser or Network Browser.

Check the network wiring that goes to both computers for loose connections, damaged cables, and proximity to fluorescent lights or other sources of electromagnetic interference.

On a LocalTalk network, check for proper termination, and make sure the daisy chain is not a closed loop, as described in Chapter 2.

You can't turn on file sharing in the File Sharing or Sharing Setup control panels.

Follow these steps until the problem is solved:

1. Make sure the computer has at least 400K available on its hard disk.

2. If the computer uses disk formatting software not made by Apple, check with the software publisher to make sure it works with file sharing.

3. In the File Sharing control panel or Sharing Setup control panel, enter a different owner name, owner password, and computer name. Then try again to turn on file sharing.

4. Drag the File Sharing folder out of the Preferences folder (inside the System Folder). Restart the computer and try to turn on file sharing.

5. Drag the Users & Groups Data File out of the Preferences folder. Restart the computer and try to turn on file sharing.

6. Reset the PRAM. You do this by restarting the Mac while holding down the Command-Option-P-R keys.

7. Open the Extensions Manager control panel; make sure the AppleShare extension is present and turned on.

8. Re-install the Mac OS; this will replace any missing or damaged files required for file sharing.

You are unable to make a folder or disk a shared item.

▼ Make sure the computer's hard disk has at least 1MB available.

▼ Remember that you can't share

- A floppy disk or its folders.
- Some types of removable disks or the folders on them. Check with the maker of the disk about this limitation.

▼ If the computer uses disk formatting software not made by Apple, check with the software publisher to make sure it works with file sharing.

Glossary

Numbers

10BaseT
A common type of Ethernet hardware that operates at up to 10Mbps, using Category 3 or Category 5 unshielded twisted-pair cables and RJ-45 connectors.

100BaseT
A common type of Ethernet hardware that operates at up to 100Mbps, using Category 5 unshielded twisted-pair cables and RJ-45 connectors.

10/100BaseT
Ethernet network adapters and hubs that can operate at both 10Mbps and 100Mbps using Category 5 cables and RJ-45 connectors.

10 Mbps
10 megabits per second, the maximum theoretical data-transfer rate, or bandwidth, of standard Ethernet.

100 Mbps
100 megabits per second, the maximum theoretical data-transfer rate, or bandwidth, of Fast Ethernet.

access privileges
The levels of user access you assign to shared files or drives on a Macintosh (similar to permissions in Windows).

adapter
See network adapter.

AppleTalk
A network protocol most often used for printer and file sharing on a network of Macs. AppleTalk is easy to set up and use. Windows PCs can use AppleTalk by installing extra-cost software.

back up
The process of making a copy of files stored on a disk for use in the event that the original files are accidentally modified, damaged, or destroyed.

bandwidth
The maximum theoretical rate at which data can be transferred between two points. For a number of reasons, including network overhead, the actual amount of data transferred never approaches the network bandwidth.

binding
In Windows, the configuration process that enables a network adapter, protocols, and network software to work together.

BNC
British Naval Connector. A type of locking connector used with coaxial cables. (Not used in 10BaseT or 100BaseT Ethernet.)

bit
Short for "binary digit," a bit is a basic unit of data in computers. A bit signifies either a 0 or a 1. (*See also* byte.)

browser
An application that enables you to look through network information casually. The Windows Network Neighborhood, the Macintosh Network Browser, and the Macintosh Chooser are browsers for a local network. Microsoft Internet Explorer and Netscape Communicator are examples of Web browsers.

byte
Typically, a group of 8 bits of data. You can think of a byte as a "digital word."

cable
A bundle of insulated wires encased in a protective sheath.

cable modem
A device that links a computer or a network to the Internet over a cable television connection. You need an account from a cable TV company or ISP to use a cable modem.

cascade
To connect Ethernet hubs together.

Category 3
A grade of unshielded twisted-pair cables and RJ-45 connectors suitable for 10BaseT Ethernet.

Category 5
A grade of unshielded twisted-pair cables and RJ-45 connectors suitable for 10BaseT or 100BaseT Ethernet.

Chooser
A Macintosh utility (accessible from the Apple menu) for selecting a printer or connecting to a shared folder or disk. The Chooser is a browser for your local network.

client
On a network user's computer, a program that makes use of shared resources on a network. The user's computer itself may also be referred to as a client.

coaxial cable
A type of cable consisting of a center wire surrounded by one or more layers of conductive mesh. Can be used for Ethernet networks, but twisted-pair cables are more popular for small Ethernet networks.

connector
A plug at the end of a cable; also, the socket, jack, or receptacle to which the plug connects.

crossover cable
A 10BaseT or 100BaseT cable in which the send and receive wires are reversed at one end. Used to connect two computers without a hub, to connect two hubs without an uplink port, and to connect some cable modems to a computer's network port.

daisy chain
A wiring configuration in which each computer or other network device is connected directly to the next computer or network device, and no hub is used.

database
An organized collection of information. Most commonly used to mean a computer file containing this information. On a network, some database software lets you share a database, letting multiple users view or change information.

dedicated server
A computer that is dedicated to the task of providing one or more types of data or services on a network; the dedicated server is reserved for network work and is not used as a primary workstation by a single person.

DHCP server
Dynamic Host Configuration Protocol. A type of server software that automatically assigns IP addresses to computers on the network.

DNS server
Domain Name Service. A type of server software that correlates a recognizable Internet (or intranet) address and its IP address; for example, www.peachpit.com and 207.149.188.79 both refer

to the same site. To set up an Internet connection, you need to know the IP addresses of your ISP's DNS servers. Also known by the more generic term name server.

driver
Software that enables communications between a computer's operating system and a hardware device such as a network adapter or a printer.

DSL
Digital Signal Line. A type of high-speed Internet connection provided by an ISP or a local telephone company. DSL connections range in speed from 128Kbps to 1536Kbps or faster. Several variations of DSL are available.

e-mail
Electronic mail. A method of sending and receiving messages among computers on the Internet or on a local network. E-mail is more advanced than messaging software, letting you manage received messages and send messages to a select group of people.

Ethernet
The most common standard for transmitting data over a local network. Many variations of Ethernet exist. Several of them, including the popular 10BaseT, transmit data at up to 10Mbps. Other Ethernet variations can transmit data faster. Ethernet works with a variety of protocols, including TCP/IP, NetBEUI, IPX/SPX, and AppleTalk.

Fast Ethernet
A form of Ethernet that transmits data at up to 100Mbps. One increasingly popular variation is 100BaseT. Fast Ethernet accommodates the same protocols as regular Ethernet, including TCP/IP, NetBEUI, IPX/SPX, and AppleTalk.

file server
A computer with specialized software that manages centralized file storage and file-sharing capabilities for everyone on a network.

file sharing
Collective use of data among the computers in a network. File sharing is included with Windows and the Mac OS.

full duplex
Communications in which both parties can transmit at the same time. A telephone call is a full-duplex communication.

group calendar
A type of database software that lets multiple users view a calendar and schedule appointments. Usually, the software lets you schedule appointments that all can see as well as those only visible to you. Also called group scheduling.

hardware
The electronic and mechanical components of a computer or add-on device.

host
The software on one network that provides a service to matching guest software on other network computers. For instance, a mulitplayer game host on one computer keeps track of the individual players on other computers.

hub
A central connection box for computers on a 10BaseT or 100BaseT Ethernet network.

Internet gateway
Computer software or a freestanding hardware device that allows all of the computers on the local network to share a single Internet connection.

intranet
A local network that uses the TCP/IP protocol and contains Internet-like services, such as a Web server.

IP
Internet Protocol. *See* TCP/IP.

IP address
The four numbers separated by periods—such as 169.254.1.1—that identify a single computer on a local TCP/IP network or on the Internet.

IPX/SPX
Internet Packet eXchange/Sequenced Packet eXchange. A network protocol used with some multiplayer game software and other network

applications. It was invented by Novell for use in large NetWare networks.

ISA
Industry Standard Architecture. An older type of expansion slot and associated electronics in PCs. ISA slots are 16-bit.

ISP
Internet Service Provider. A company that provides users with a connection to the Internet through a regular modem, cable modem, ISDN modem, DSL, or another type of link.

IRQ
Interrupt ReQuest. A type of low-level setting on a PC that designates a communications path from a piece of hardware, such as a network adapter, mouse, or monitor, to the PC's motherboard. Adjusting the IRQ setting is rarely required for modern Plug and Play–compatible computers and network adapters, but it may be necessary for older hardware.

ISDN
Integrated Services Digital Network. A type of high-speed communications service used for connecting computers to the Internet or for other purposes. Data rates for ISDN typically range from 56Kbps to 128Kbps.

kilobit
About one thousand bits of data—to be exact, 1,024 bits of data, or 2 to the 10th power (2^{10}).

Kbps
Kilobits per second. Data transfer speed measured in multiples of 1,024 bits per second.

LAN
Local area network. *See* local network.

local network
Two or more nearby computers connected together to share documents, programs, equipment, and/or services. (Also known as a local area network, or LAN.)

local printer
A printer that connects to a computer, which may in turn share the printer with other computers on the network.

LocalTalk
An older network hardware system for Macintosh and some printers that connects through serial ports. The most common LocalTalk hardware uses inexpensive connector boxes and ordinary telephone cords to connect in a daisy chain. LocalTalk works only with the AppleTalk protocol and transmits data at up to 230.4Kbps, or 0.225Mbps.

mapping drive letters
The process in Windows of assigning an unused drive letter (such as E:, F:, or G:) to another computer's shared folder or drive. Once mapped, this network drive is treated as a local disk drive.

megabit
About one million bits of data—to be exact, 1,024 kilobits, or 1,048,576 bits, 2 to the 20th power (2^{20}) of data.

Mbps
Megabits per second. Data transfer speed measured in multiples of 1,048,576 bits per second.

messaging
A network service that allows network users to carry on impromptu written conversations via their computers. Usually an incoming message pops up instantly on the recipient's computer screen.

modem
Short for *modulator/demodulator*. A device that transmits and receives digital signals over telephone lines by converting them to and from analog signals (sound waves).

multiplayer game
Game software that accommodates two or more players over a network.

N

name server
See DNS server.

NetBEUI
An easy-to-configure network protocol included with Windows. Can be used for sharing printers and files on a small network but not for multiplayer games. (Macs can use NetBEUI only with the installation of extra-cost software.)

network
A means of connecting computers and other devices to enable communications among them, such as sharing printers and files and sharing an Internet connection.

network adapter
An internal or external device that enables a computer to participate on a network. Also known as a network interface card (NIC). *See also* network adapter card and PC card.

network adapter card
When installed inside a computer, the network adapter card enables the computer to participate in a network. Also known as a network interface card (NIC).

Network dialog box
The Windows dialog box where you set up networking for a PC, accessible from the Control Panel.

network drive
See mapping drive letters.

network interface card (NIC)
See network adapter card.

Network Neighborhood
In Windows, the desktop icon that, when clicked, shows network computers and their shared printers, folders, and disks. The Network Neighborhood is a "browser" for your local network.

network path
In Windows, the location of a shared printer, disk, or folder on a network computer; expressed as the computer name followed by the name of the shared printer, disk, or folder. For example, the path \\Ned's PC\Public refers to the shared folder named Public on the computer named Ned's PC.

network printer
A printer that connects to a network just like the network computers that may use the printer.

network service
A component of one computer that does work for other computers on a network. More specifically, in Windows, Network Services is the name of the software that enables a PC to share its printers and files with other network PCs.

network software
Software that enables computers and other devices to communicate and to share services and resources on a network.

NIC
Network interface card. *See* network adapter card.

node
A computer, network printer, or other network device that has its own network address (such as an IP address). An Ethernet hub, however, is not a node.

notebook computer
A self-contained, battery-powered, full-featured computer about the size of a thick notebook of letter paper. Also known as a laptop computer.

 P

parallel port
A standard port on PCs, most often used to connect a local printer. Called *parallel* because data is sent along multiple wires simultaneously.

patch cable
A cable with plugs at both ends.

PC
Personal computer. As commonly used, a desktop or notebook computer based on an Intel or compatible processor, most often running the Windows operating system. Although a Macintosh is in fact a personal computer, it is not usually referred to as a PC.

PC card
An expansion card about the size of a credit card that slides into an external opening found primarily on notebook computers. Formerly known as PCMCIA card.

PCI
Peripheral Component Interconnect. A type of internal expansion slot found in most desktop Windows and Macintosh computers.

PCL
Printer Control Language. The most common language used to control printers and to specify the content of pages to be printed. It was invented by Hewlett-Packard.

peer-to-peer network
A network of computers that look to each other for services and shared resources rather than looking to a dedicated server.

permissions
In Windows, the levels of user access that can be assigned to shared files or disks on a PC.

phone-line network
A network hardware system that uses special network adapters and ordinary telephone wires. The initial HPNA (Home Phone Network Alliance) standard for phone-line networks achieves a maximum data rate of about 1Mbps and uses the same protocols as Ethernet, including TCP/IP, NetBEUI, IPX/SPX, and AppleTalk.

Plug and Play
A feature of Windows 95 and Windows 98 that simplifies the configuration of newly installed hardware. Plug and Play technology eliminates the need to manually adjust low-level settings, such as IRQs and memory address lines. (A similar capability has long been part of Mac OS.)

port
As commonly used, a connection point on a computer or on a device that connects to a computer. A port can also be a virtual connection point, such as a file, or an abstract connection point, such as the COM and LPT ports in Windows.

PostScript
A language commonly used on high-quality printers for precisely describing text and graphics placement on a page. It was invented by Adobe Systems.

power-line network
A network hardware system that uses special network adapters and electrical power lines to transmit data at a top rate of 350Kbps.

protocol
The rules of communication that computers use to share a service or resource on a network. Specific protocols include TCP/IP, NetBEUI, AppleTalk, and IPX/SPX.

printer language
The language a computer uses to control a printer and specify the content of pages to be printed: for example, PCL (printer control language) and PostScript. A printer can support one or more printer languages. On the computer, the print driver determines the printer language used.

proxy server
A feature in Internet gateway software that acts as a go-between for the computers on a network and for the servers on the Internet. Instead of requesting Web pages, e-mail service, and other Internet services directly, all your networked computers request the services from the gateway's proxy server.

R

RJ-11
The type of plugs and jacks used to connect a telephone to a wall jack and to connect the most common kind of LocalTalk network connector boxes.

RJ-45
The type of plugs and jacks used to connect a 10BaseT or 100BaseT Ethernet network.

router
A hardware device or software that forwards traffic from one network to another using a particular protocol, such as TCP/IP traffic from a local network to the Internet. Internet gateways often include a router.

S

self-assigned IP addresses
A feature of Windows 98 and Mac OS 8.5 and later; enables computers to give themselves non-static IP addresses without the existence of a DHCP server.

serial port
A type of computer port that sends data one bit at a time. Commonly used for a modem, keyboard and mouse, a PC, and some Macintosh local printers.

server
Software on a computer that provides a particular kind of data or service on a network. A computer that runs server software is also referred to as a server, especially if it is not a user's personal computer.

share
In Windows, a shared folder, disk, or printer.

shared folder
A network computer's folder to which other network computers can connect.

static IP address
A manually entered IP address that's not subject to change.

software
A program or system of programs that enables a computer to perform a particular task.

subnet mask
A number that determines which part of an IP address identifies the network and which part identifies a computer on the network. For example, the subnet mask 255.255.0.0 specifies that the first two numbers of an IP address identify the network and the last two numbers in an IP address identify a particular computer on the network. On a small local network, all the computers should have the same subnet mask.

T

TCP/IP
Transmission Control Protocol/Internet Protocol. The network protocol used on the Internet. It is widely used on local networks as well.

twisted-pair cable
A type of cable consisting of pairs of twisted wires mutually encased in a protective sheath.

W

Web server
A specialized program that serves up Web pages requested by Web browsers on the Internet or on a local network.

wireless network
A network hardware system that uses special network adapters and radio or infrared waves to transmit data at top rates of 1.6Mbps, 1Mbps, or 0.5Mbps, depending on the brand of hardware.

Index

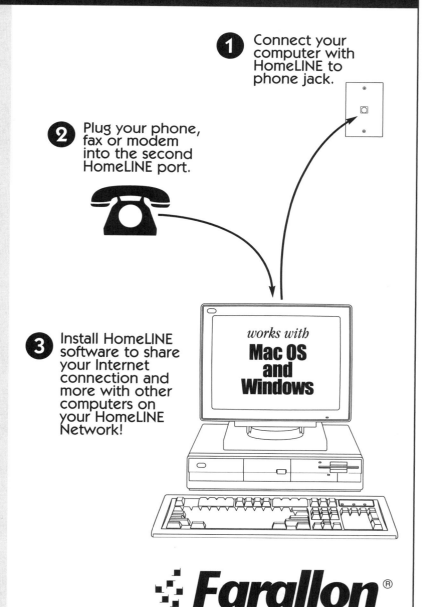